WORDS OF A
GOOD SHEPHERD

The Life, Ministry, and Inspirational Messages
of the Reverend Dr. Otis L. Hairston, Sr.

Compiler—EMMA HAIRSTON BELLE

With Foreword by the Rev. Nelson Johnson

WESTBOW
PRESS
A DIVISION OF THOMAS NELSON

WestBow Press books may be ordered through booksellers or by contacting:

WestBow Press
A Division of Thomas Nelson
1663 Liberty Drive
Bloomington, IN 47403
www.westbowpress.com
1-(866) 928-1240

ISBN: 978-1-4497-5926-1 (hc)
ISBN: 978-1-4497-5927-8 (sc)
ISBN: 978-1-4497-5928-5 (e)

Library of Congress Control Number: 2012914286

Printed in the United States of America

WestBow Press rev. date: 08/16/2012

Contents

Part IV: Selected Editorials, Writings, and Speeches

Part V: Reprint of a Manual for Pulpit Search Committees in Baptist Churches By Otis L. Hairston Sr.

For my mother, Anna C. Hairston

FOREWORD

One of the great blessings of my life was to serve with the Rev. Dr. Otis L. Hairston Sr. during the last three years (1989-92) of his long, illuminating pastorate at Shiloh Baptist Church. I arrived in Greensboro, North Carolina, in 1965. Nineteen years later in 1984, during one of the most difficult periods of my life, my wife, Joyce, and I joined Shiloh. I was moved to join Shiloh because I heard the compassionate Word of God being preached, and I experienced a measure of the love that is God within the Shiloh church family. I was called into the Christian ministry two years later and entered seminary in the fall of 1986. When I graduated from the School of Theology at Virginia Union University, the Rev. Hairston invited me to serve at Shiloh as assistant to the pastor. I was honored and happily accepted. I found him to be a strong, but gentle, leader. I stress "strong and gentle" because far too often, the trait of meekness (which Jesus calls blessed) is thought of as weakness. Nothing could be further from the truth.

As you read this magnificent book, you will experience in the sermons preached by the Rev. Hairston the meekness, clarity, and penetrating faith that characterized his ministry. You will discover in these pages Otis Hairston the pastor, the social justice advocate, the community leader, the nurturer, and the reconciler. You will also experience the warmth, care, and loving touch of family members who compiled this portrait of his life. As I read the introduction, sermons, editorials, and various speeches, my appreciation of the Rev. Hairston grew even more, as this book gives us a glimpse from multiple perspectives of this dedicated servant of God.

The Rev. Hairston's sermons had power. They were powerful, not because he was the greatest orator, but rather because the sermons had relevant ethical teachings, spiritual depth, compassion, and biblical integrity. His messages spoke pointedly to the needs of the mind, body, and soul. In his sermon "Is Life Worth Living?," a message that appears to be no more than ten minutes in length, he graphically describes the discouragements, frustrations, and despairs of life that push so many to the brink, questioning whether life is worth living. But with compelling simplicity, this sermon cuts through the fog and helps the listener see how much God loves us, that God is for us, and that "we can have faith in His trustworthiness." His messages make it clear that "when all around our soul gives way, He is our hope and stay." These pages are packed with such powerful, relevant, and spiritually grounded messages.

As a pastor, the Rev. Hairston modeled what it means to be a "good shepherd." Jesus taught us that "the greatest among you will be your servant" (Matt. 23:11 MLB). The desire to serve, to care for his members and the community was very strong in the Rev. Hairston. He not only visited the sick and counseled those in need of guidance who were members of his church, but he also routinely visited and provided counsel for others who were not members of Shiloh. The story is told that the Rev. Hairston, on more than one occasion, convinced the medical staff when he was hospitalized to allow him to leave the hospital to serve communion to his congregation and then return to the hospital. On one occasion, the Rev. Hairston found himself hospitalized when he was scheduled to marry a couple from out of town. They very much wanted the ceremony to be performed by the Rev. Hairston. Therefore, he invited the couple to come to the hospital to take their vows there, an invitation that they happily accepted. The Rev. Hairston showed us what it means to be a pastor and, indeed, a Christian servant-leader.

The Rev. Hairston was a leader for social justice, and his voice was heard over a span of some sixty years as he spoke up and stood up for the dignity, worth, and unrealized potential of all humankind. He was not afraid to speak to the vast racial injustices that were everywhere apparent during his lifetime. He understood well the centrality of justice to the Christian message. The Rev. Hairston wrote a brief but persuasive article in 1956 titled "Segregation." The meaning of that message, less than one page, is not tainted by time, for it is rooted in the timeless principles of justice. On the Martin Luther King Jr. holiday of 1996, four years after his retirement as pastor of Shiloh, the Rev. Hairston gave a speech at the Crescent Rotary Club that is a beautiful summation of his sense of social justice. In this speech, he acknowledged the social progress stubbornly won through struggle; however, he also made clear the challenges of all the work yet undone. He expressed all of this in a spirit of reconciliation and healing. We would all benefit from his example of persisting in the important work of social justice.

The Rev. Hairston exemplifies what it means to be a father and a devoted family man while being committed to a demanding vocation. Males, black males in particular, could reap an immense harvest from his positive example. While this book does not explicitly engage the question of family and fatherhood, it is nevertheless sprinkled throughout these pages in the form of sermons, writings, and examples. It is a common saying that when one marries a preacher, both the spouse and the preacher are called to the ministry. I am sure Anna Cheek Hairston, the Rev. Hairston's loving wife of fifty-eight years, could attest to this profound truth. I am equally sure that they both added value to each other in their beautiful journey together.

I shall always be grateful to the Rev. Hairston for giving me the opportunity to serve and learn under his leadership. I am also thankful that some of the life lessons and the spiritual inspiration of his leadership are captured in the pages that follow. Indeed, the Rev. Hairston lived the poem he recited every first Sunday, the last stanza of which says:

> Others, Lord, others;
> Let this, my motto be.
> Help me to live for others
> That I might live like thee!

I know this book will be a blessing to all who read it. It will be a special blessing to the many generations who came of age under the pastorate of the Rev. Otis L. Hairston Sr.

Rev. Nelson N. Johnson
Pastor, Faith Community Church,
Greensboro, North Carolina
March 26, 2011

PREFACE

Shortly after my father, Dr. Otis L. Hairston Sr., passed away on July 18, 2000, I began to go through some of his old papers and came across some handwritten sermons and writings. It amazed me how he put such care into organizing and keeping meticulous records of his sermons and activities as a minister. My father's words spoke to the hearts of his congregation in the pews of Shiloh Baptist Church. It was his words that inspired the Greensboro Four to be the spark that began the sit-in movement in the 1960s. What truly amazed me about my father was not just the words that he preached, but his actions, which gave life to those words. A visionary and a man before his time, he was never satisfied to sit on the sidelines of history, but he was compelled to use his gifts, talents, and skills to serve God and others. He truly was a "living sermon."

I realized that it wouldn't be enough to tuck away these handwritten sermons and writings in a box for safekeeping. What better way to pay tribute to him and his legacy than to put these handwritten sermons and writings into a book? I truly believe that his sermons and writings are timeless. Too often in this day and time, the words that our leaders speak, whether religious or political, are separate from the lives they live. We all can learn from a man who not only talked the talk but walked the walk.

Words of a Good Shepherd can serve as an inspiration to a seminary student, a young preacher, or any Christian who seeks to understand the life of a fellow humble Christian servant who dedicated his life to social justice, to educating our youth, the poor, and the downtrodden.

As I typed these handwritten sermons, I found that the work was very therapeutic and helped me through the grieving process after losing my father. I take comfort every day, knowing that the power of his words is still with me. He touched so many lives while he was living. And although he is not physically here with us, my hope is that my father's ministry, his powerful sermons, and his uplifting ministry will continue to inspire those who read this book.

I would like to thank my two wonderful daughters, Wanda and Monica, who helped to organize the sermons and my father's writings; my uncle, Charles A. Cheek, who helped with the typing; my mother, Anna Hairston, who helped with the editing of the book; and my husband for his support.

My deep gratitude goes to the Rev. Nelson Johnson for writing the foreword for the book and the Rev. Dr. Richard Adams and the Rev. Dr. Douglas E. Summers for their constructive feedback and encouragement.

I would like to thank my talented brother, professional photographer Otis. L. Hairston Jr., who provided the photographs that are included in this book.

Finally, to the staff of Westbow Press, I would like to extend my sincere thanks for the support, the advice, and suggestions for this project.

This book is dedicated to my beautiful and loving mother, Anna C. Hairston, who was married to Dr. Otis L. Hairston Sr. for more than fifty-eight years and walked with him during his Christian journey. It was a journey filled with love, grace, and faithfulness.

LIST OF ABBREVIATIONS

(Biblical References)

Good News Translation	GNT
King James Version	KJV
Living Bible Version	LBV
Modern Language Bible	MLB
New English Bible	NEB
New International Version	NIV
Phillips Modern English	PME
Revised Standard Version	RSV
The Living Bible	TLB
Today's English Version	TEV

PART I

THE MAN AND HIS LEGACY

INTRODUCTION

He was a leader and a preacher
But foremost he was a teacher.

A man of wisdom, courage, and determination;
Steadfast in his faith, firm in his convictions.

He spoke for all humanity
With humility and dignity.

He fought for the downtrodden and poor
So that all people would have a chance to
Knock at opportunity's door.

He was a drum major for equality and peace.
His hope for a just world will never cease.

His righteous victory has been won.
His name and legacy will live on.

—Monica Belle

The Rev. Otis Lemuel Hairston Sr., D.D., was widely known throughout the state of North Carolina as a Baptist preacher and civil rights leader. He was born April 28, 1918, to the Rev. John Thomas and Mrs. Nancy Wright Hairston in Greensboro, North Carolina. Otis was the oldest of four children. He had two brothers, Elmer and Warren, whom he loved dearly, and a sister Nancy, whom he adored. Otis grew up in the Warnersville community of Greensboro, where the beacon of hope that greatly shaped his life, Shiloh Baptist Church, is located.

House in Warnersville where Otis and his siblings grew up.

He was raised under the wise and powerful leadership of his father, the Rev. John T. Hairston, who led the church with distinction for fifty-three years. Otis accepted the mantle and call to serve at Shiloh after his father passed away, and humbly served there for thirty-four years.

When Otis and his siblings were growing up in downtown Greensboro, they were exposed to a system of segregation that separated blacks and whites in every area of their lives, from drinking fountains with glaring signs, one for whites and one for blacks, to restrooms, entrances to buildings and restaurants, and even buses, where blacks were forced to sit at the back. This system of Jim Crow, as it was sometimes called in the South, was instituted to degrade blacks and make them feel inferior to whites.

This would have been devastating had it not been for the strong values, sense of pride in their heritage, and encouragement to always do their best that were taught to Otis and his siblings, the church, and community by the Rev. J. T. Hairston. He always instilled in them that segregation was unjust.

Otis' parents—Rev. J.T. and Mrs. Nancy W. Hairston

Otis grew up in an environment where certain demands were made of people when they came to the house. His father had principles. When people came to collect insurance and wanted to keep their hats on, he would say to them, "You have to take off your hat if you want to come in here." He demanded respect in his home. He would not permit them to call him by his first name. He would insist that "if I call you *mister,* you respect me and call me *mister."* At times, his father would have to turn people away because they didn't want to remove their hats.

The attitude back then was that you didn't have to respect black people. If whites wanted a favor or to enter his house and talk to him, they had to show him respect. He demanded that, so Otis grew up instilled with the attitude of a father who demanded certain things and wouldn't accept certain things.

Otis and his siblings were very fortunate to be able to attend J. C. Price Elementary School (where his mother taught until her death in 1931) and Dudley High School. The fine teachers who took an interest in Otis, and the friendships he made while growing up in these schools, along with the nurturing he received in the church, had a profound impact on him and greatly shaped his life and true commitment to God, family, education, and community.

When Otis graduated from Dudley High School, he moved to Raleigh, North Carolina, to attend Shaw University. He quickly became active there. He helped start an effort to keep young black students from going up in the balcony in theaters, instead having them boycott theaters. Students from two of the colleges in Raleigh (Shaw University and St. Augustine College) refused to go up in the balcony to see a movie. There were no demonstrations in Raleigh, but refusing to go to the movies had an economic impact on some of the theaters. His two brothers, Elmer and Warren, and sister, Nancy, later joined him at Shaw, and for two years all four were there together. This was very important during this time because for blacks, the only way for advancement and opportunities was to seek higher education. The Rev. J. T. Hairston worked very hard and sacrificed to ensure that his children had this opportunity.

Left to Right: Otis, Warren, Nancy, and Elmer at Shaw University

While at Shaw, Otis majored in journalism. He immersed himself in the fabric of the university and became intimately involved in student life. He was the president of the Choral Club, worked as editor of the *Shaw Journal*, was elected president of the Social Science Club and senior representative to the Student Council, was a member of the YMCA Cabinet, Junior Interviewer, and a member of the Shaw University Double Sextet. His hard work and dedication earned him recognition, and he was listed in the 1939-40 issue of *Who's Who Among Students in American Universities and Colleges*.

Otis received his bachelor's degree from Shaw in 1940, and the university later awarded him an honorary doctor of divinity degree.

It was at Shaw where Otis met the love of his life and his future wife, Anna Esther Cheek, from Wise, North Carolina.

Otis and Anna at Shaw University

On June 18, 1942, Otis married his college sweetheart, and they shared fifty-eight years together and were the parents of two children, Emma Lois Hairston Belle and Otis L. Hairston Jr.; four grandchildren, Otis L. Hairston III, Wanda M. Belle, Monica W. Belle, and Warren Sidney Hairston; and one great-grandson, Jaden Alexander Hairston.

—From left—Anna, Otis, Jr., Otis holding Monica and standing Wanda and Emma

—From left—Otis, Otis III, and Otis Jr.

—From left—grandson Otis III, son Otis Jr., and grandson Sidney

—Grandson Otis III and great grandson Jaden

They made their home in Raleigh, where Otis was editor of the *Baptist Informer*—the state publication of the General Baptist State Convention of North Carolina—from 1941 to 1958 and supervisor and manager of the Baptist Supply Store from 1946 to 1958. From 1952 to 1960, he served as pastor of Brookston Baptist Church in Henderson, North Carolina.

In 1958, he became assistant pastor of Shiloh Baptist Church in Greensboro, where his father had served as pastor for more than fifty years. After his father passed away in 1960, Otis was called as pastor to serve Shiloh. When Otis retired in 1992 after thirty-four years, the congregation bestowed on him the beloved title of pastor emeritus.

There was no pretense in Otis Hairston. He was very humble, modest, authentic, and genuinely loved people. He sought no fame and glory in Greensboro or in any place he went. He just wanted to honor God through his words and deeds. He was truly respected for what he did in his church and throughout the community. His modesty and humility were characteristics that endeared him to anyone who came into contact with him and to his cherished friends and family. The Rev. Hairston did everything in his power to make his dream of a better world a reality. He supported the call for nonviolence by Dr. Martin Luther King Jr. in the 1960s. Many lives were touched, and this world was truly made a better place because he lived.

The Rev. Hairston was on the forefront of the civil rights movement in Greensboro in the 1960s, encouraging four young men to be the spark that began the sit-in movement. One of the four young men grew up in Shiloh, and the pastor opened his office in the church so the students could use the mimeograph machine to make copies. During that time, he received death threats at his home as well as bomb threats at the church. He received a phone call late one night requesting him to come out to a house to counsel a family facing a crisis. If he didn't come, he was told, something bad would happen. He thought about going because of his willingness to help people, but his wife talked him out of it. The next day he drove out to the address and discovered it was an abandoned house in a wooded area.

When the Freedom Riders came through Greensboro and were attending a rally at Shiloh Baptist Church, the Rev. Hairston heard the phone ring in his office. The caller made a bomb threat. This was a common tactic used to try to disrupt civil rights meetings. The meeting would break up because the police would clear the building to search for a bomb, and the attendees would go home because of the long wait. The Rev. Hairston hung up the phone, returned to his seat, and kept the call a secret.

Despite the threats and danger during that time, the Rev. Hairston remained steadfast and continued to stand up for mankind. As noted in an article by Nancy H. McLaughlin in the Greensboro *News & Record* on July 19, 2000, two days after his death:

> The Rev. Otis Hairston Sr. was thought to be one of the key reasons Greensboro, birthplace of the sit-in movement, didn't explode in violence in the 1960s as did Selma or Birmingham, Ala. "There were people who wanted to be destructive. He kept a lot of things from happening that even I couldn't as mayor," said Carson Bain, who served as mayor during the late 1960s. "He has left quite a legacy." Bain said Hairston often set up meetings between the mayor and black people who were angry over Jim Crow practices. "He diffused a lot of tensions that could have led to violence," said Bain, who met with Hairston in the hospital two days before he died.
>
> Later, another Greensboro mayor, Jim Melvin, also sought Hairston's advice. "He was such a calming influence, was not shy, was really known to take on tough assignments and truly was a perfect example of living a sermon," Melvin said. "He was a great man and should go down as one of the truly great leaders of our town."

While serving on the school board, the Rev. Hairston would often be spat upon as he left meetings. His goals while serving on the board were to see that all students had the opportunity for quality education regardless of where they lived and regardless of their race.

The Rev. Hairston said that he always felt sorry for people who were prejudiced and that you had to love them and keep praying for them. He worked to change white people's attitudes about black people.

He was a charter member of the original Greensboro Human Relations Commission in 1963, president of the Greensboro Ministers Fellowship (1966-67), president of the Greensboro Citizens Association (1963-64), membership chairman of the NAACP (1961-63), and president of the Pulpit Forum (1958-63).

The Rev. Hairston served in positions on many other local, state, and national boards. They are as follows:

- Recording secretary, General Baptist State Convention
- Assistant recording secretary, Progressive National Baptist Convention, Inc.
- Chairman of the Administrative Committee, General Baptist State Convention
- Chairman of the Personnel Committee of the General Baptist State Convention
- Member of the Executive Committee of the Council of Review, State Democratic Party
- Greensboro Board of Education
- Board of Trustees, Bennett College
- Board of Trustees, Shaw University
- United Way Board
- Chamber of Commerce Board
- United Day Care Board
- Hayes-Taylor YMCA Board
- Industries of the Blind Board of Directors
- Advisory Board, Greensboro National Bank
- Chaplain on call, Wesley Long Hospital

An extremely modest man, the Rev. Hairston was the recipient of many honors and awards. In 1966, he was named a Ford Fellow, receiving a grant to study urban missions at the Urban Training Center for Christian Missions in Chicago.

In 1974, the *Carolina Peacemaker* newspaper named the Rev. Hairston as the recipient of its second annual Peacemaker award. He was selected on the basis of his undying efforts to aid the community in whatever manner necessary. "As a record of how busy Rev. Hairston is, he preached 57 sermons at Shiloh last year (1973). Also included in his totals for last year are 209 visits to hospitals and nursing homes, two visits to prisons, 17 addresses and sermons elsewhere and 16 state and national conferences and meetings attended," the *Peacemaker* noted on April 13, 1974. The award was presented to him by Dr. J. Marshall Stevenson, editor of the *Peacemaker*, in ceremonies at A & T State University. In presenting the award, Stevenson noted that it was given to the "citizen who has done most for the advancement of peace at home and in developing interracial understanding and brotherhood in our region."

In 1979, the Tau Omega Chapter of the Omega Psi Phi Fraternity honored the Rev. Hairston as Citizen of the Year. As a civic leader, he had served on thirty-eight boards and commissions throughout the city, state, and nation.

On September 13, 1981, Governor James B. Hunt conferred the Order of the Long Leaf Pine upon the Rev. Hairston with the title of ambassador extraordinary privileged to enjoy all rights granted to members of this exalted order.

On November 14, 1982, Dudley High School, from which the Rev. Hairston graduated in 1936, dedicated a black studies library collection in his honor. He was a member of the Greensboro Board of Education from 1971 to 1979.

In 1983, the Rev. Hairston was honored by the Greensboro chapter of the National Conference of Christians and Jews. He was awarded the chapter's 1983 Brotherhood Citation following an address by Governor Hunt and an introduction by Rep. L. Richardson Preyer of the Sixth Congressional District. Hunt called the Rev. Hairston "a leader of strength and faith." Preyer praised him as a person who lived by his church's motto: "Shiloh cares about people. He has taken his caring and turned it into doing," Preyer said. "A modest man who always credits others for his success, he has remained true to his commitment to brotherhood over the years. He has been an ambassador for human rights, an advocate of tolerance and decency, a defender of the downtrodden," the *Greensboro Daily News* said on October 5, 1983.

Rev. Hairston receiving Brotherhood Award from former
U.S. Rep. L. Richardson Preyer.

In December 1992, the Greensboro Chamber of Commerce presented the Levi Coffin Award to the Rev. Hairston for leadership in human rights, human relations, and human resources development in Greensboro.

On August 23, 1994, the Greensboro Exchange Club enrolled him in its Book of Golden Deeds.

Some of the other awards bestowed upon him were:

- Distinguished Alumni Award, Shaw University, 1990
- Friend of Bennett Award, Bennett National Alumnae Association, 1990
- NAACP Man of the Year Award, 1978
- Distinguished Service Award, North Carolina Council of Churches, 1983
- Listed in *Who's Who Among Black American Leaders,* 1981
- Listed in *Who's Who in the South and Southwest,* 1968
- Listed in *Personalities of the South,* 1984
- Listed in *Black American Clergy,* 1989

Upon the Rev. Hairston's death on July 18, 2000, the Greensboro City Council passed a resolution honoring his memory.

In April 2001, almost a year after his death, the Guilford County Board of Education named a new Greensboro middle school after the Rev. Hairston. The Otis L. Hairston Sr. Middle School is located near Franklin Boulevard in east Greensboro.

Otis L. Hairston, Jr. (son) and Otis L. Hairston III
(grandson) standing in front of school sign.

The Rev. Hairston loved the Warnersville community and dedicated his life to service in trying to give back to those in need. During his life, he saw many changes in the community, the economic hardship that people faced, increases in crime, and the lack of programs for youths and seniors. He envisioned developing a central place in the community in connection with the church where necessary programs could be provided and youth and seniors could connect—a family life center. Shiloh decided to honor this vision and worked diligently for many years to bring this dream to fruition. In April 2010, a groundbreaking ceremony was held for the first phase of the O. L. Hairston Sr. Family Life Enrichment Center, and on March 27, 2011, a dedication ceremony took place.

From Left standing—Wanda, Emma, and Monica at groundbreaking
ceremony in April 2010 for phase one of Family Life Center

12/26/2011

Otis L. Hairston, Sr. Family Life Enrichment Center

PART II

THE CALL TO SHILOH AND ITS MINISTRIES

THE CALL TO SHILOH

On Sunday, August 7, 1960, Otis Hairston was installed as pastor of Shiloh Baptist Church after being elected as successor to his father, J. T. Hairston, in April 1960. The Rev. J. T. Hairston was called to lead Shiloh on May 10, 1907, and served until his sudden death from a heart attack while working in his study in February 1960. Under the elder Hairston's leadership, the second church building was erected in sections—an educational wing in the early 1930s during the Depression and the worship section in the late 1940s. The church grew from fewer than one hundred members to a membership exceeding five hundred. Beginning in March 1958, Otis had served as assistant pastor. The congregation's leaders quickly asked Otis to succeed his father. After taking a month to think about it, he agreed to become pastor.

In the poem "Others," Charles D. Meigs relates the motto that Otis Hairston lived by and recited every first Sunday during communion.

> Lord, help me live from day to day
> In such a self forgetful way
> That even when I kneel to pray,
> My prayer shall be for others.
>
> Help me in all the work I do
> To ever be sincere and true
> And know that all I'd do for you,
> Must needs be done for others.
>
> Let "self" be crucified and slain
> And buried deep, and all in vain
> May efforts be to rise again
> Unless to live for others.

And when my work on earth is done
And my new work in heaven's begun
May I forget the crown I've won
While thinking still of others.

Others, Lord; yes, others;
Let this my motto be.
Help me to live for others
That I might live like Thee.

This is the motto that the Rev. Hairston tried to instill in his congregation. He once said, "The way you measure worship is not what happens in this building, but what happens when people go out of it in terms of their involvement in making life better for other people."

The Rev. Hairston was never satisfied with business as usual. He always instructed the congregation to remember that the biggest "room" in the church is the "room for improvement." Worship services were designed to equip members to move from the church building to be Christian servants in the world outside. Music was basic to the Shiloh worship experience. There were six choirs—three for youths and young adults and three for adults—an instrumental ensemble, and a hand bell choir.

Under his pastorate, Shiloh was:

- The first Greensboro church to sponsor a summer enrichment program for underprivileged children, serving sixty children ages six to ten beginning in 1968.
- The first North Carolina Church to sponsor housing for low-income families.
- The first minority church to establish a scholarship fund for high school graduates. (The fund was begun in 1961 as a memorial to the late Rev. J. T. Hairston. Graduates from the church and community have been awarded scholarships ranging from $150 to $3,500).
- The first Greensboro minority church to sponsor and provide space for an AA group, beginning in 1978,

WORDS OF A GOOD SHEPHERD

- The first Greensboro minority church to sponsor Little League baseball teams for boys in public housing.

In addition to these pioneering firsts, Shiloh provided meeting space for striking sanitation workers in the 1970s and for the Freedom Riders in the 1960s.

John 10:14 NIV says, "I am the good shepherd; I know my sheep and my sheep know me." Just as the good shepherd sacrificed himself for a helpless herd and laid down his life for his sheep, so did the Rev. Hairston sacrifice himself for his Shiloh family and the community. God used him to show others the way—to encourage members to reflect Jesus Christ in their lives, both inside and outside the church.

The Rev. Hairston always made a point of being there when members needed him—at the hospital when they were sick, on call when a loved one died, and willing to listen whenever they had a problem. He always said, "They need you at that particular moment, when it's a crisis. The next day isn't a crisis." He was there even if it meant getting up in the middle of the night. On one occasion, he was in the hospital himself when he was scheduled to perform a marriage ceremony for a young person who had grown up in the church, moved away, and come back to Greensboro to be married. The Rev. Hairston had his wife bring him a suit from home. He received permission from his doctor to have the nurse remove the IV and oxygen and wheel him to the hospital chapel (he was a chaplain on call at the hospital), and he performed the ceremony there.

When the Rev. Hairston was a patient in the hospital and it was communion Sunday, he would talk the doctor into giving him a three-hour pass so that he could go to church and serve communion to his congregation, returning to the hospital after the service.

THE IMPORTANCE OF MEETING HUMAN NEEDS

> For I was hungry and you gave me something to eat, I was
> thirsty and you gave me something to drink, I was a stranger
> and you invited me in, I needed clothes and you clothed me,
> I was sick and you looked after me, I was in prison and you
> came to visit me.
>
> —Matt. 25:35-36 NIV

The Rev. Hairston always said, "Salvation is not only for the future.
It's for here on earth and now." Under his pastorate this philosophy
took Shiloh Baptist Church into the community and opened the doors
of the church to those who could benefit from its help. The church's
slogan was "Shiloh cares about people." Its definition of *church* was and
is that the church building is an equipping station and the members
who make up the church fellowship are Shiloh Baptist Church. Worship
services attempted to equip members to move from the church building
into the world to be servants by becoming servants of God.

While still in its old building, Shiloh became the first church
in Greensboro to enter the low-to-moderate-income housing field,
becoming the nonprofit sponsor for 108 apartment units.

The following is an excerpt taken from a booklet written by the
Rev. Hairston. titled *The Shiloh Housing Story*:

> In several of His parables and other teachings, Jesus
> emphasized the importance of meeting human needs.
> During His earthly ministry, He demonstrated His concern
> for the disadvantaged. In fact, the beginning of His public
> ministry was marked by the reading from the book of the
> prophet Isaiah 61:1-3 NIV: "The spirit of the Sovereign

Lord is on me, because the Lord has anointed me to preach good news to the poor. He has sent me to bind up the brokenhearted, to proclaim freedom for the captives and release from darkness for the prisoners, to proclaim the year of the Lord's favor."

It is made clear in Matthew 25:31-46 that the Lord of the universe will not judge nations and persons on the basis of religious knowledge, fame, reputation, church work, or even great verbal testimonies, but by how they have responded to meeting human needs.

For sixty or more years, Shiloh's church building was located in the center of a community surrounded by substandard housing. It was common for rats to come up through holes in the floors, for soiled mattresses to be used as beds, and for rooms to be flooded with water during rainy periods. The "landlords" showed no real interest in improving or correcting these disgraceful dwellings on which they collected rent. City government failed to pursue courses that would demand that the owners bring these "shotgun" houses up to a level of decency.

Appeal after appeal was made to city government to condemn the houses that failed to meet the standard requirements of the city itself. The response was always the same, "We will look into the complaints."

After a year of appealing to city government without any action, a committee was formed from the church and the community to secure the names of slum landlords with houses in the area of the church and to appeal to them to improve the conditions of the houses that they rented. To the surprise of the committee, most of the "slum" landlords were involved in city government.

From the 1940s through the 1960s, rental houses were, for the most part, sources of supplementary income for the owners. They invested in substandard houses to "make money." There was no deep concern about the conditions of the houses they rented. As long as they could collect rent, they were apparently satisfied. They resented "outsiders" complaining about the conditions of houses that they didn't occupy.

Attempting to move beyond criticism and protest, Shiloh Church leadership initiated a study in the early sixties on ways the church could become viably involved in helping to improve housing the church community. The church felt an obligation to do more than preach about the "golden streets" in heaven. The church wanted to help provide some comfortable and healthy living conditions for people in this present world.

Fortunately, Shiloh was approached in early 1964 about its interest in becoming a sponsor of housing for low-income families under a new federal rent supplement program with a Federal Housing Authority guaranteed loan.

On February 5, 1964, some officers and a committee met with Mr. Robert E. Barkley, executive director of the Redevelopment Commission of Greensboro, to discuss the possibility of the church developing apartments for low-income families in the Warnersville neighborhood. It was revealed that a new government program known as 221D housing had just been approved by the U.S. Department of Housing and Urban Development (HUD). With encouragement from Mr. Barkley and Mr. Fairley, assistant to Mr. Barkley, the church voted to apply for sponsorship of a 221D program under the auspices of the 1963 National Housing Act.

The 221D program was designed to assist private nonprofit organizations in construction of housing for low-income families. Under the program such families pay 20 percent of their income for rent, and HUD supplements the remainder needed for the standard rental rate in the housing project. The beauty of the 221D program is that as a family's income increases, the amount of rent it pays is increased and the supplement reduced. It differs from public housing in that, when the income of a family reaches a certain level, the family does not have to move. It merely pays its own way.

After extensive study and discussion of the new program by the pastor, officers, and members, a church conference was held on December 12, 1965, to formally vote on a recommendation by the deacon and trustee boards that the church form a nonprofit corporation to apply to HUD for sponsorship of 221D housing for low-income families. Following a period of questions and answers, the congregation voted unanimously to approve the recommendation of the deacon and trustee boards.

The congregation also voted that the proposed housing project would be named the J. T. Hairston Memorial Apartments in memory and honor of the deceased pastor who served Shiloh from 1907 until his death in February 1960.

On March 6, 1967, the pre-application was submitted to the Federal Housing Administration for the construction of apartments on an 8.5-acre tract at Marsh Street and Freeman Mill Road. The pre-application was subsequently approved, and the church was instructed to proceed with its plans.

The drawings had been prepared by Mr. Clinton E. Gravely and Associates prior to the pre-application, and were submitted with the application.

The initial closing was held in November 1968. Approval was given by the Federal Housing Administration for construction of 108 units and an administrative-Laundromat building at a cost of $1,195,500. The apartments were designed to include sixteen one-bedroom units, sixty two-bedroom units, twenty-six three-bedroom units, and eight four-bedroom units.

Groundbreaking for the complex was conducted on November 24, 1968, and the first units were occupied in December 1969. All of the units are all-electric, centrally heated and soundproofed. Play lots have since been developed along with a community fellowship building and a storage facility for equipment. Before families could move into the project, they first had to take classes in homemaking, budgeting, and community living. The reason for this is to develop a community, not just to provide housing. At the outset of the project, Shiloh was concerned with doing more than just "putting a roof over the heads" of residents. The church was committed to building a community and developing self-worth and dignity among the residents. As a consequence, the church underwrote the salary of a part-time social worker who would assist in developing the social fabric of the community and help residents with problems associated with receiving benefits from public agencies, housekeeping, nutrition, and budgeting. The person would also initiate programs to enrich the lives of the residents.

In October 1971, a groundbreaking ceremony was held for the current church building at 1210 S. Eugene Street.

Ground-Breaking Scene with Shiloh Baptist from
1925-1973 in background

On August 1, 1973, the new Shiloh Baptist Church opened its doors. The new church building gave the membership an opportunity to broaden the scope of service even more.

The Rev. and Mrs. Hairston standing in front of sign of
new church building

In October 1973, a day care center for sixty children ages three to
five years was opened in the new church building. The children took
part in an instructional program and were cared for while their parents
were at work. The day care center had an AA rating from the state
for twelve years. The church also operated an after-school program for
twenty-four years.

A scout room enabled the church to offer a complete scouting
program for boys and girls, three groups in dramatics, three groups
in creative exercises, basketball teams for youths and adults, and
special senior citizen activities. In 1980, the church was recognized
by the Baptist Association on Scouting, based in Nashville, Tennessee,
as having one of the outstanding scouting ministries among Baptist
churches in America.

The dramatics groups provided an opportunity for teenagers to
develop their talents in drama and public speaking. Plays and pageants
were presented to church gatherings and the public. Every fourth
Sunday, the youths participated in the morning services by reading the
responsive reading and giving the prayer.

A library was established for members and the community.

The church had a paid director of social services who coordinated social outreach programs and projects and helped meet a variety of needs of members and persons in the church community. A weekly program was conducted for senior citizens and a summer enrichment program for disadvantaged youths.

Two buses were operated by the church to bring worshipers to Sunday school and the Sunday morning service. The bus also was used for transportation of scouts and senior citizens and for general youth activities.

Provisions were made for anyone needing to visit a doctor or hospital to get there. Persons who had no way to pick up surplus food were given transportation, or a designated person would go for the food and deliver it.

A supply of food was kept in a storeroom at the church to fill emergency needs. The church had an account at a local department store to take care of emergency clothing needs.

When the Rev. Hairston retired after thirty-four years, he retired from the pulpit, but not from work. He continued to work for causes that concerned him.

PART III

INSPIRATIONAL MESSAGES

HANDLING LIFE'S ADVERSITIES

In the world you will have trouble: but have courage! I have overcome the world.

—John 16:33 MLB

Life does not give us all that we want. Life is not a bed of roses. No religion can guarantee us smooth sailing down life's highway. There are many adversities to be encountered simply in living. Some days we are up and some we are down; some days we have our joys, and some our sorrows. There are days of success and days of failure, days when the winds are calm and days when the winds are reckless. Though life brings many pleasant and thrilling moments, it also brings hardships, disasters, and disappointments. There are days of laughter and days of weeping.

Christ informs His disciples in our text that adversities will be a part of life in this world. "You will," He said, "find trouble in the world." As a wise teacher and an honest friend, He prepares His followers for life as it will be faced in the world. He would make it clear to us that we cannot live without adversities, but we must learn to live in spite of them.

Adversity is not necessarily an evil. Listen to the apostle Paul writing in Romans 5:3-4 KJV: "And not only so, but we glory in tribulations also: knowing that tribulation worketh patience; and patience, experience; and experience, hope."

Because of adversity, understanding, patience, endurance, and sympathy can be learned. Wounded souls can bring wonderful blessings.

We cannot sing the great hymns of the church without being reminded that many have come from the pens of persons in adverse conditions.

Fanny Crosby, blind from childhood, wrote some eight thousand songs. Comforting words from her pen inspire millions during rainy days. Such as:

> All the way my Savior leads me,
> Cheers each winding path I tread
> Gives me grace for every trial,
> Feeds me with the living bread.
> Though my weary steps may falter,
> And my soul athirst may be,
> Gushing from the rock before me,
> Lo! A spring of joy I see.

Our meditation hymn was written by a woman burdened down with seemingly unbearable sorrow. Despondent, she wrung her hands and cried repeatedly, "What shall I do? What shall I do?" Suddenly, her face lit up and she exclaimed, "I must tell Jesus." The words were put together by Elisha Hoffman.

> I must tell Jesus all of my trials;
> I cannot bear these burdens alone;
> In my distress He kindly will help me;
> He ever loves and cares for His own.
> I must tell Jesus! I must tell Jesus!
> I cannot bear my burdens alone,
> I must tell Jesus! I must tell Jesus!
> Jesus can help me, Jesus alone.

The apostle Paul gives us classic words concerning the proper attitude we should adopt in the face of adversities: "We know sorrow, yet our joy is unquenchable. We have nothing to bless ourselves with, yet we bless many others with true riches. We are penniless, and yet in reality we have everything worth having."

With the proper attitude toward adversities, we can move on to develop uncrushable courage. Jesus would have us first understand that we must not lose heart because of adversities. Paraphrasing the words of Paul in 2 Corinthians 4:8-9, we may be handicapped on all sides, but we must never be frustrated; we may be puzzled, but we must never despair; we may be persecuted, but we must realize that we never have to stand it alone.

In our adversities, we must not throw up our hands and cry, "What's the use?," but must, as Jesus ordered us, have courage.

Christ, almost a total failure with His own beloved people, went gracefully to the cross with undiminished love and unconquerable faith in God and won the victory over the adversities of the world. He bids us because of his victory: have courage.

MAKING MUSIC ON LEFTOVERS

Let everything that breathes praise the Lord.
—Ps. 150:6 RSV

Be watchful, and strengthen the things which remain.
—Rev. 3:2 KJV

Several years ago, there was distributed to hospital patients a booklet with meditations especially directed to those who were deeply depressed in their sickness. One of the striking meditations dealt with learning to live with troublesome limitations that sickness so often brings about.

The booklet related the story of a great violinist who had the A string snap just as he reached the climax of a concert. He didn't stop the concert, but finished the piece on the three remaining strings. He made music on leftovers.

Many people today in the course of life's concert will have their A strings snap. If they make music, they must make use of what remains.

In every community there are many who live with some kind of handicap. Basically, there are two ways people respond when life's A string snaps. Some will stop making music. They will spend valuable time complaining about the misfortune. They eventually lose faith in themselves and in the enabling power of the universe. They become bitter.

Many people are defeated with the loss of a limb, or the loss of relatives on whom they depend for security, or the loss of health or wealth. When the A string snaps, life's concert ends.

However, there are others who respond not by complaining and becoming bitter, but who with inspiring courage from the enabling power of the universe continue life's concert. They strengthen what remains and make their music. They refuse to say, "There I go with the loss of a limb, or relative, or health, or wealth." Life to them is tied up with a spirit that is within and yet beyond. They continue to sing praises to their creator.

Our real security is never in legs, arms, eyes, voice. We can lose all of these and still be secure. We can have all of these and still be insecure. Security is never in that which is destructible.

What we need in our afflictions is not a question answered . . . we need the God who is beyond time and above troubles. We need to know that the heavenly Father, who keeps His eyes on the flying sparrow, watches us. When we cling to Him, the music never ceases. We glorify Him when losses occur. We sing with the psalmist:

> Praise ye the Lord . . . Praise Him for his mighty acts;
> Praise Him according to His excellent greatness.
> —Ps. 150:1-2 KJV

God can take away and give us greater power after loss.

There is always left after our losses the real person. There is God who exalts the valley, brings low the mountain and hill, and makes rough places plain. There is left the God who lifts us above all handicaps and puts a song in our soul when the shadow darkens and the sun is eclipsed. Losses can cause many to stop the concert before it is finished. Keep on playing with what remains.

WHEN THE STORMS OF LIFE BECOME VIOLENT

So keep up your courage, men, for I have faith in God
that it will happen just as He told me.
—Acts 27:25 NIV

Paul was being carried to Rome by ship to be placed in jail. The ship set out during the winter season and faced many storms at sea.

One storm became so violent that all but Paul felt certain that the ship and all of those on it would be destroyed.

When all of the crew had given up hope and their despair was clear to Paul (the prisoner), he stood up and said, "Men, take courage! For I trust in God."

There are not only storms at sea that become violent and get out of hand and cause us to despair, but there are storms in life that become violent and cause us to despair. There are troubles in life that we cannot cope with. We are helpless so often against the crushing blows of affliction.

The violent storms are always beyond our control. There are some storms that we can find shelter from.

At times we get ourselves into trouble through our carelessness. We get entangled in messes that we overcome through mere will power.

Mistakes are sometimes made that we are able to correct and avoid violent suffering.

Some of life's storms we can handle ourselves. On the other hand, life sometimes brings storms that we cannot handle. They are beyond our control. They are violent and threaten to destroy us.

What shall we do when the storms of life become violent? Real deliverance comes in life's violent storms. We don't have to get the ship out of the violent sea. God is in the midst of the violent storms, and

He is able to deliver the ship in the storms. As the songwriter Charles Albert Tindley says in the hymn "Stand by Me,"

> When the storms of life are raging,
> Stand by me (stand by me);
> When the storms of life are raging,
> Stand by me (stand by me);
> When the world is tossing me
> Like a ship upon the sea
> Thou Who rulest wind and water,
> Stand by me (stand by me).
>
> In the midst of tribulation,
> Stand by me (stand by me);
> In the midst of tribulation,
> Stand by me (stand by me);
> When the hosts of hell assail,
> And my strength begins to fail,
> Thou Who never lost a battle,
> Stand by me (stand by me).
>
> In the midst of faults and failures,
> Stand by me (stand by me);
> In the midst of faults and failures,
> Stand by me (stand by me);
> When I do the best I can,
> And my friends misunderstand,
> Thou Who knowest all about me,
> Stand by me (stand by me).
>
> In the midst of persecution,
> Stand by me (stand by me);
> In the midst of persecution,
> Stand by me (stand by me);
> When my foes in battle array
> Undertake to stop my way,
> Thou who savèd Paul and Silas,

Stand by me (stand by me).

When I'm growing old and feeble,
Stand by me (stand by me);
When I'm growing old and feeble,
Stand by me (stand by me);
When my life becomes a burden,
And I'm nearing chilly Jordan,
O Thou "Lily of the Valley,"
Stand by me (stand by me).

He is our unfailing companion.

All along life's pilgrim journey.
He will lead us thro' the vale of shadows,
He will bear us o'er life's fitful sea
Then the gate of life eternal,
We can enter in with Him.
—Fanny Crosby

CHEER UP! BELIEVE GOD!

Next to Jesus, the apostle Paul is the most dominating figure in Christianity. Of the twenty-seven books in the New Testament, Paul wrote fourteen. He is portrayed as a poet on love, a philosopher on immortality, a theologian on the nature and person of Christ, an adviser and organizer of churches, an instructor, and a counselor.

He lifted Jesus as not only Savior, but as Lord and Master to whom we need to surrender ourselves in order to find new life. Paul leads us out upon that path of true redemption and hands us over, prisoners, to Christ. He points at the truth that sets the prisoner free. "Therefore if any man be in Christ, He is a new creature" (2 Cor. 5:17 KJV).

After persecuting the Christians, he was converted while traveling down the Damascus road. From that day, he became Christianity's boldest witness of the gospel of the grace of God. He was persecuted for proclaiming the gospel, but he kept on telling the good news of God's redeeming love through Christ; he was beaten, but he kept on telling the good news; he was placed in prison, but he never ceased telling the good news.

He preached at Damascus where he was converted. When he came to Jerusalem, where he was educated, he continued to bear witness to God's grace manifested in the death and resurrection of Jesus. He witnessed throughout all the coasts of Judea. He preached to the Gentiles and pleaded with them to turn to God—turning from that which was evil to that which was good.

Arrested for his preaching the gospel of the resurrection of Jesus, he was brought before King Agrippa. He preached so convincingly before the king that the king was almost persuaded to become a believer.

Paul requested to be taken to Rome and tried by Caesar. He had written to the Romans: "So, as much as in me is, I am ready to preach the gospel to you that are at Rome also. For I am not ashamed of the gospel of Christ: for it is the power of God unto salvation to everyone that believeth; to the Jew first, and also to the Greek" (Rom. 1:15-16 KJV).

King Agrippa would have perhaps dismissed charges against the apostle Paul, but agreed, at Paul's insistence, to have him carried to Rome to appear before Caesar.

The trip to Rome was a long voyage. They encountered great difficulties as they set out. After reaching Fair Havens, Paul warned the captain that the journey should not be continued until winter was past. Winter was a dangerous time to travel the seas. Paul was overruled, and the ship left Fair Havens.

As Paul had warned, the storms at sea made it impossible to control the direction the ship sailed. For many days, neither sun nor stars appeared. The storm got worse. All hope was lost that the ship and crew could be saved.

After days of silence, Paul stood up in the ship and first reminded the crew of his advice against sailing from Fair Havens in the winter. Then he bided them to cheer up and believe God. "There stood by me this night the angel of God, whose I am, and whom I serve, saying, Fear not, Paul; thou must be brought before Caesar: and, lo, God hath given thee all them that sail with thee" (Acts 27:23-24 KJV).

He had something inside him that caused him to rise above circumstances. Paul did his best to change the circumstances. The lesson is that we ought to try to avoid sailing against the adverse winds of life. We should try to change the circumstances, try to avoid the stormy seas.

But when we have tried our best to avoid bad situations, and find ourselves helplessly facing adverse winds of life, then we trust in God to lead us safely through the stormy seas.

When things are at the breaking point, and we have done all that we can do, we must lean upon God.

Paul believed that when God commissioned him for a task, God would see him through. He could trust God to plant his footstep on the sea and ride upon the storm.

It is the kind of faith that will lead us to see a cloudy sky and know that the sun will come out by and by. It is facing the dark night of trouble and knowing that the light will in time break forth. It is whistling when engulfed in blackness. It is singing at midnight with a rope around our necks. It is seeing no way out of bad situations and yet believing that God will make a way.

These are dark days for our nation. We are traveling stormy seas. We face many adverse winds. We need to do all we can to avoid bad situations.

When we have done all that we can do, we need to lean upon God.

> We need a faith that shines bright and clear
> When tempests rage without,
> That when in danger knows no fear,
> In darkness feels no doubt.
> Lord, give me such a faith as this;
> And then, whate'er may come
> I'll know while here, the hallowed bliss
> Of my eternal home.
>
> —William Hiley Bathurst

God is real. We have a great God.

FACING THE FUTURE

> I don't mean to say I am perfect. I haven't learned all I
> should even yet, but I keep working toward that day when I
> will finally be all that Christ saved me for and wants me to
> be. No, dear brothers, I am still not all I should be but I am
> bringing all my energies to bear on this one thing: forgetting
> the past and looking forward to what lies ahead.
>
> —Phil. 3 12-13 TLB

Wouldn't it be wonderful if we would face the future with the kind
of excitement, determination, and faith expressed by the apostle Paul? I
heard one of our deacons say at deacons' retreat yesterday that God was
not through with him yet, a quote which expresses the determination
that God still has something for him to do.

Several weeks ago, I came across an announcement that the late Dr.
E. Stanley Jones, famous missionary to China and India, made on his
seventy-fifth birthday.

With confidence, he announced that the next ten years would be
the best years of his life. A week or so later, I said to one of my pastor
friends, "I'm determined that the next five years will be the best years of
my life and will also be the best years for Shiloh." He replied, "Suppose
your life is cut off on earth before?" My reply was: "They will still be
the best five years in my life because what lies ahead after death is even
better."

As we face the unforeseeable future, our determination ought to
be to bring all our energies to bear to make the future our best months
and years.

What a blessing would come to us and to the church if we would
resolve that the best of life is not behind but ahead! That we would have
the determination of the apostle Paul: "I haven't learned all I should

42

even yet, but I keep working toward that day when I will finally be all that Christ saved me for and wants me to be."

William Carey, an English missionary, who was one of the early leaders of the Baptist Church, preached a sermon after being turned down by associations to support missionary endeavors in Africa titled "Attempt Great Things for God and Expect Great Things from God."

No doubt, God is anxiously waiting for some of us to forget what is behind and to look forward in faith to the blessings that lie ahead. Many of us cannot move forward for looking back—some looking back at failures, others looking back at successes. Paul had written fourteen books of the New Testament and had set one of the finest examples as a servant of the living Lord that had been seen, and yet he says that "forgetting the past and looking forward to what lies ahead, I strain to reach the end of the race and receive the prize for which God is calling us up to heaven because of what Christ Jesus did for us" (Phil. 3:13-14 LBV).

God is not through with me yet.

I challenge you today—as you face the unforeseeable future—to resolve that the year 1985 will be your best year and that you will do your best to make it so. "Attempt great things for God and expect great things from God."

It is so easy for us who have been around a few years—and now our steps are slowing down—to say that our best years are behind. God is not through with us yet. The best here on this earth could still be ahead.

Likewise, young and old argue, why should I look forward to a bright future when things ahead don't look promising? The answer is that the future is not uncertain or without promise of being the best because it belongs to God. The heroes of faith trusted God to bring to pass the things they hoped for.

Noah, ignoring the mockery of others, took God at His word and built an ark, and was saved from destruction. God's message looked foolish to others, but Noah believed it and staked everything on the Word of God.

Sarah, at ninety (the best years behind), was past the age to conceive and bear a son, but she believed God, and Sarah bore a son to Abraham—Isaac.

Abraham, at an age when many assume that the best years are behind and God is through with them, was called by God to go to an unknown land. He obeyed and left his homeland, and God kept the promise that a great nation would be established, that his name would be great, and that all peoples on earth would be blessed through him. God was not through with Abraham!

Face the future not with fear, but with faith! Assume the positive attitude about life.

Don't spend your time worrying about the bad things that could happen; hope and prepare for the best!

The best is ahead! God is not through with you yet!

Let's give our best in making this church all that Christ wants it to be.

I'm determined to make the next year or the next five years my best years. They will be my best years—living or dead. If God sees fit to take me home before, that's His business.

There is one thing that I courageously trust in. Though the heavens fall and the earth caves in, I am convinced like that gifted servant of Christ who found both meaning and joy in his life serving his Lord. Here are words written to that little band of believers in Rome:

> For I am persuaded, that neither death, nor life, nor angels, nor principalities, nor powers, nor things present, nor things to come, nor height, nor depth, nor any other creature, shall be able to separate us from the love of God, which is in Christ Jesus our Lord.
>
> —Romans 8:38-39 KJV

The best is ahead! Praise the Lord!

IS LIFE WORTH LIVING?

There is no fear in love. But perfect love drives out fear.
—1 John 4:18 NIV

If God is for us, who can be against us?
—Rom. 8:31 NIV

We are more than conquerors through Him who loved us!
—Rom 8:37 NIV

Several weeks ago, a young man stood on the ledge of a bridge, threatening to jump off. Some years back, a twenty-five-year-old man stood on the eighteenth-floor ledge of a hotel on Fifth Avenue in New York for eleven hours. He was spotted by the noonday crowds on their way to lunch. He was standing between two windows that opened onto the ledge spaced in such a manner that he could not be reached. If anyone attempted to go out of the window after him, he threatened to jump. It was an agonizing day of suspense. Through the afternoon, he smoked cigarettes and waited. Thousands waited on the street below to witness the death of a fellow creature. Relatives and friends, including his sister and former classmates, psychologists, priests, and ministers, went to the window and pleaded with the young man. He quietly smiled, and said, "I want to be left alone."

After dark, the floodlights were turned on. A friendly patrolman went to the window and begged him to come off. He replied, "I wish someone could convince me that life is worth living." Shortly thereafter, he leaped to his death.

Thirty thousand people in our country will take their lives this year because they will conclude that life is not worth living.

They will include students who after great effort will fail examinations; lovers who are betrayed by their lovers; persons convicted of embarrassing crimes; brokenhearted mothers and fathers; wealthy people who have lost their riches; healthy people who have lost their health. There will also be those who find life leading to a dead-end street.

Even good people find it difficult to have courage when life's choicest hopes crumble, when cherished friendships are broken and loved ones are hushed in death. It's not easy to stand up to life when life's clouds engulf us and when it seems that all around our soul gives way. It's not easy to have courage when earthly joy and beauty fade.

The question is asked: is life worth living?

The best of us have moments of discouragement, disgust, frustration, and despair when we need to be reminded that God loves us. Even when earth borne clouds of darkness surround us, we are surrounded by a love that will not let us go. Because God loves us, life is worth living. All else can appear against us, but God is always for us.

We need to be firmly grounded in faith to stand up to life. God is for us, and we can have faith in His trustworthiness. When all around our soul gives way, He then is all our hope and stay. When we have faith in God's love, life is meaningful and worth living.

In 1 John 4:18 RSV, we are told that "perfect love cast out fear." Nothing can pluck us out of the Father's hand. Nothing can separate us from His love. He can dispel the clouds of darkness and reveal His light.

He is not only the creator of the boundless universe, but He is a friend beside us on life's perplexing highways and seas. Because He is beside us, we can face bitter moments of life.

THE CHANGELESS CHANGER

Jesus Christ is the same yesterday and today and forever.
—Heb. 13:8 RSV

Therefore, if any man be in Christ, he is a new creature: old things are passed away; behold, all things are become new.
—2 Cor. 5:17 KJV

We have in these two verses two distinctive claims of Christianity. No other religion can claim to have as its founder and leader a changeless person—nor a person who can change the old into the new.

Our religion offers to the world one who is unchangeable amidst a changing world. He is the same in a world that is constantly changing.

The world is always changing. Change and decay all around we see—governments, city, schools, family life.

However, in the face of all of the changes, there are some things in our world that are unchangeable. The mountains stand tall with strength and majesty, reaching into the blue heavens with the enduring qualities of the eternal hills.

The waves of the sea continue to wash against the beach in quiet motion or in thunderous billows, echoing the melodious music of the deep. These unchangeables are not subject to the modifications of man, but are a part of the very structure of the earth itself.

It is in a world built in such depth that faith is developed in the One who changes not. Isaac Watts expresses this faith in the following verse:

Before the hills in order stood,
On earth received her frame,
From everlasting Thou art God,
To endless years the same.

The Christian faith is rooted in a person who is beyond time—the same yesterday, today, and forever.

Though He is changeless, His mission is always to change. The prophet Isaiah in chapter 40:4 KJV warned that before His coming, "Every valley shall be exalted, and every mountain and hill shall be made low: and the crooked shall be made straight, and the rough places plain."

After his death, John the Revelator, in Revelations 21:1 NIV could write: "Then I saw a new heaven and a new earth, for the first heaven and the first earth had passed away."

The mission of this great changeless one is to change unholy structures. Listen to His own words in Luke 4:18-19 KJV: "The spirit of the Lord is upon me, because he hath anointed me to preach the gospel to the poor; he hath sent me to heal the brokenhearted, to preach deliverance to the captives, and recovering of sight to the blind, to set at liberty them that are bruised, to preach the acceptable year of the Lord."

When His Spirit moves into the structure of governments, businesses, churches, and homes, a great change takes place. Justice rolls down like water, and righteousness as an ever-flowing stream.

This truth has been true in the past; it is true today; it will be true through eternal ages. The changeless Christ transforms the life of nations. History attests to this transforming power. When nations fail to abide by the principles of Christ, there is disorder. Confusion and decay set in.

Christ's mission is not only to change the nations, but to transform unholy structures through new people. The apostle Paul gives us the Word when he writes: "If any man be in Christ, he is a new creature: old things are passed away; behold, all things are become new." The past attests to this fact. New life came to all those of yesterday who permitted Christ to come into their lives.

That changeless Christ is changing the lives of men today. Men are being lifted from the gutters of life; the spiritually blind and lame are having their eyes opened and legs strengthened. Men are still being taken out of the miry clay and put upon a rock to stay; the bruised are being healed; the dumb are singing; the sick restored; the dead resurrected.

"If any man be in Christ, he is a new creature." Redeemed people still sing, "What a wonderful change in my life has been wrought."

THE IMPOSSIBLE IS POSSIBLE

In the nineteenth chapter of the gospel of Matthew, we have an account of Jesus' encounter with a rich young ruler. The young man approached Jesus with the question: "Good Master, what good thing shall I do, that I may have eternal life?" (Matt. 19:16 KJV). After an extensive examination of the man's knowledge of the law and a look into his heart, the Master instructed the young ruler to go and sell all the wealth he possessed and give to the poor and he would have riches in heaven. Thinking of his great possessions, he refused to follow the advice of Jesus, going away sorrowfully. Whereupon Jesus said to His disciples, "Verily I say into you, that a rich man shall hardly enter into the kingdom of heaven . . . It is easier for a camel to go through the eye of a needle than for a rich man to enter into the kingdom of God" (Matt. 19:23-24 KJV).

Amazed and disturbed at the sayings of their Master, the disciples asked the question: "Who then can be saved?"

Jesus replied: "With men this is impossible; but with God all things are possible" (Matt.19:26 KJV).

In our day, when men are limiting the power of God to change them and the world, we need an unfaltering trust in an all-powerful God who is vast, limitless, and transcendent. One who can reach to the ends of His world and move into any situation with a hand that is strong and mighty. Our God is the one who still keeps the stars in the universe, moving in endless rhythm in the trackless skies, and the tiny blade of grass by the roadside. He is the one who openeth rivers in mountains and fountains in the midst of the valleys. He brings princes to nothing and maketh the judges of the earth as vanity.

The Bible everywhere holds that with God all things are possible, for everything is under His control. What is impossible with man is always possible with God.

Jesus went out of His way to prove that, by prayer, man could achieve what is seemingly impossible. He went as far in His teaching as to say that the very mountain on which the city stood could be removed into the sea by the prayer of a person of sufficient faith. What He was emphasizing is that we must not limit God. Our world, with its conflicts and sufferings, needs to know that though it is impossible for humanity to save itself, it is possible for the God who created the world to reach down and deliver helpless men from desperate plights.

To his doom, modern man with his so-called intellect limits God. Our prayers are powerless because deep down within us, we cannot believe that "All things are possible with God." We fail to pray for physical miracles because we feel that the natural laws cannot be broken. Though it may not be our intention, we put what God has created above God.

Often we pray with the conviction that the universe operates without a mastermind behind it. We have the feeling that our universe operates simply on a mechanical order. If the universe is strictly mechanical, then miracles cannot occur. If miracles cannot occur, we may as well stop talking about a supernatural being. *Supernatural* means that God is above the natural. We worship Him because we believe He is supernatural. God is the maker and sustainer of the universe. He is the Lord of the universe and Lord of natural laws. He created the natural (body, mind, and soul).

If mountains are not moved, it is not because God cannot move them, but because we fail to believe that "all things are possible" and therefore we limit God.

The only limitation on God is the limitation we put on Him with our weak and faltering faith. Remember what Jesus said to the father who brought to Him the son with the dumb spirit. "If thou canst believe, all things are possible to him that believeth" (Mark 9:23 KJV).

Of course forgiveness is a condition we must meet.

The second is faith—faith that goes out into the darkness believing that a light will appear; moving out into the river, believing that when our footing slips, a hand will reach out and grip ours.

Mountains are moved through faith.

WHEN TRIALS COME

Count it all joy, my brethren, when you meet various trials, for you know that the testing of your faith produces steadfastness.

—James1:2-3 RSV

James, the brother of Jesus, points out that religion is something to be practiced. He insists that righteousness involves performance.

In our text, he offers a different view concerning trials. Trials, which most men regarded as evils to be avoided, are looked on as something Christians ought to accept joyfully. It is through trials, the apostle would argue, that we grow into strong and enduring soldiers in the army of Christ. So he writes, "Count it all joy . . . when you meet various trials."

Every person needs a test. A person who tries to avoid trials that test his strength is attempting to run away from life. Life is made up of trials. No man lives without trials. He is born unto trouble as the sparks fly upward. He must face sickness and death. He must meet disappointments.

Trials serve as tests for us. They are like examinations for students. An examination determines how well the students have taken in what has been taught by the teacher. It is actually a test for the teacher as well as for the students. Trials in life determine how much Christians have grown like their Master and teacher.

Tests are means of proving our preparedness or lack of preparedness. A person spends sixteen or twenty years in school preparing for a vocation. The test comes when he leaves school and goes out into the world to put his learning into practice.

Teachers are required to do practice teaching. The doctor is required to serve as an intern.

It would be silly to spend a third of one's life preparing to do something, and when the time came to perform, the person avoids performing.

The football player is anxious to be called off of the bench and sent into the game to perform. It is through performing that he is put to the test. He cannot prove to the coach that he is a good player until he gets out on the field and plays. Likewise, the baseball pitcher is anxious to get out on the mound to demonstrate his ability.

James is saying that when a Christian is faced with various trials he should rejoice, for he is being presented an opportunity to play in the game of life and prove his strength. He develops and proves his strength not by avoiding the tests but by facing them. Therefore he is to count it all joy.

A ship must be able to ride a storm. There is no other way than storms to test the workmanship. Trials are the only way to test growth and strength.

When a man is applying for a job, one question almost sure to be asked of him is, what's your experience? What it amounts to is: have you been tested?

Tests are used to determine promotions. Soldiers are promoted in the army when they have proved their ability (through performance). So God promotes soldiers in His army when they have demonstrated their growth. "Count it all joy when trials come," for we have a chance to get a promotion to move up a little higher.

The strength of Jesus was shown as He faced His trials. One of His greatest tests came in the wilderness when Satan tempted Him to use his great power for personal ends. Jesus suffered hunger rather than turn stones into bread. Bread was not to be the center of His seeking. "My meat is to do the will of him that sent me, and to finish his work" (John 4:34 KJV).

Our various trials can be used as a means of testing. The Christian is put to a test through his suffering.

A rabbi, commenting on the text "The Lord trieth the righteous" (Ps. 11:5 KJV), said, "The potter does not test the cracked vessels. It is useless to tap them even once, because they would break. He does, however, test the good ones, because no matter how many times he taps them they do not break."

As tests are not merely for the students but for the teacher, so our testing benefits the great teacher. The reason Jesus pleads for us so earnestly in the hour of trials is that our triumph is His triumph. Every time a Christian meets a test, not only can he rejoice but Christ rejoices. The son who becomes a prodigal is glad to get back home, but he is not half as glad as the father. When a student succeeds, naturally he rejoices, but the teacher rejoices as much, for the victory of the student is as much the victory of the teacher. So it is with our great teacher and Master.

Finally, when we face trials, we should rejoice because it is only through enduring the trials of life that we can receive the crown of life. "Blessed is the man who endures trial, for when he has stood the test he will receive the crown of life which God has promised to those who love him" (James 1:12 RSV).

What a wonderful experience to be given any kind of crown. People work hard for earthly crowns that perish. The great crown is the crown of life bestowed by Christ. It is not a pie-in-the-sky type of crown that we receive when we die, but the crown of life. It is a crown of acceptance—accepted by Christ as a good and faithful servant—to be told that you have stood the test.

WHEN WE BELIEVE IN GOD

Only a fool would say to himself, there is no God.
—Ps. 53:1 TLB

Belief in God makes a difference in how we live and how we die.

Let us start by pointing out three things that happen to those who don't believe in the God who is creator and sustainer of life.

1. They never find real purpose in life.
2. They never live as persons but as things and have no sense of lasting moral law value.
3. They have no hope of tomorrow.

Belief in God is essential for purposeful living. God is He without whom we cannot live. Without belief in God, there is nothing that gives meaning and purpose to life. God is the reality on which life is built. When we believe in God, we recognize that there is a mighty mind at work in the universe, one who is an engineer, an artist, and a father.

A great engineer to structure the physical universe so that it stays intact. The sun, the moon, and stars never fail to shine. A mighty mind to create a universe with beauty on every side: springtime and autumn, summer and winter, sunrise and sunset, mountains at sunrise, valleys in moonlight.

A great artist or mastermind to create generations of creatures and to know them all by name and even know the number of hairs on their heads.

A great father who never slumbers in caring for His creation.

When we believe in God, we find purpose in life. As St. Augustine said, "He made us for Himself and our souls are restless until we rest in Him." When we believe in God, we live as persons, not as things. Whenever we push God aside, we make a sorry mess of life. Whenever we go our own way, we go wrong.

God is He without whom men cannot live. God is not an elective in the school of life. He is a requirement. Everything goes wrong without Him. Life is empty without Him. Only God gives us an abiding sense of value. Like coins, men have value, not in themselves, but because they bear the stamp of the King. A coin, to be worth anything, must have stamped on it the inscription of a government. We are children of God because we have been stamped by God.

Finally, when we believe in God, we believe in tomorrow. God sets eternity in our souls.

LOVE YOUR ENEMIES!

You have heard that it hath been said, Thou shalt love thy neighbor, and hate thine enemy. But I say unto you, Love your enemies, bless them that curse you, do good to them that hate you, and pray for them which despitefully use you, and persecute you; that you may be children of your Father which is in heaven; for he maketh his sun rise on the evil and on the good, and sendeth rain on just and on the unjust.

—Matt. 5:43-45 KJV

Do not repay anyone evil for evil. Be careful to do what is right in the eyes of everybody. If it is possible, as far as it depends on you, live at peace with everyone. Do not take revenge, my friends, but leave room for God's wrath, for it is written: "It is mine to avenge; I will repay," says the Lord. On the contrary: If your enemy is hungry, feed him; if he is thirsty, give him something to drink. In doing this you will heap burning coals on his head. Do not be overcome by evil, but overcome evil with good.

—Rom. 12:17-21 NIV

The slaves were able to interpret the religion of Jesus far better than their masters. When they sang that great spiritual "Lord, I Want to Be a Christian in My Heart," they were expressing the central desire of those seeking to be Christ like—"a Christian in my heart."

To be a real Christian, one must be a Christian in the heart; that is, to have an experience that is felt, and not something that has been merely heard or read about.

Nicodemus wanted only to be a Christian in his head, but Christ demanded religion of the heart.

The Christian way emphasizes the change of a person's heart as primary. Certainly Christ was concerned with the whole man, but He realized that unless the heart was pure, the other parts would be defiled.

Without religion of the heart, we cannot live up to the demands of Jesus to love. In no uncertain terms, He called upon His followers to love those who say and do all kinds of unholy and evil things about us and to us. Love is to be the garment that robes His disciples. He demands of Christians to love enemies, bless them who curse, do good to them that hate, and pray for them which despitefully use us—in order to be children of the Father. We don't grow like our Father who is in heaven unless we grow in love for all people.

Why must we love enemies?

1. Jesus commanded it as a means of keeping before us the fact that an enemy is still a brother. When we deal with an enemy, we are dealing with our brother—it is only his animosity and bitterness that make him our enemy.
2. Love is the great soul force that leads our enemies to respond favorably to us and through which we win them as friends. Jesus put the matter plainly: "How can Satan drive out Satan?" (Mark 3:23 NIV). Can you, by acting like the devil, get the devil out of people? You cannot get rid of darkness by going out fighting with your fist. You can only overcome hate with love.
3. Paul points out that love for all those in the fellowship is the only principle strong enough to bring unity to the church. The church was created and it is maintained by love. Love underlies the whole of God's redemptive activity. It is the secret of all that God has done for us. In the fellowship, we must not only learn to sympathize with those who are at odds with us when they are in sorrow, but must learn to rejoice when they succeed or find joy. "And above all these, put on love, which binds everything together in perfect harmony" (Col. 3:14 RSV).

4. We punish ourselves when we attempt to punish our enemies with revenge. There is no peace with hatred in our hearts. Paul said, "Do not take revenge, my friends, but leave room for God's wrath, for it is written: It is mine to avenge; I will repay" (Rom. 12:19 NIV). "Recompense to no man evil for evil." (Rom.12:17 KJV). God still orders this world that He made. "Be not deceived, God is not mocked: for whatsoever a man soweth, that shall he also reap" (Gal. 6:7 KJV).

5. Loving our enemies, we must believe in them. Perfect love casteth out all fear. Hate is against life. It is against goodness. It is against rightness. It is against God. It destroys the mind. It disintegrates the spirit. It blocks our communion with God.

There is no peace with hatred in our hearts. God is the source of strength. Love for enemies is impossible without God's strength. Give me power to forgive my enemy and love Him.

THE PURPOSE OF IT ALL

The coming of Christ was to reveal the light and love of God. God comes to be with us.

Why did He have to come? What was the purpose of it? To redeem man; to deliver him from the sin that had destroyed life. Sin separates us from God. We become embarrassed, naked, and conscious of our nakedness (Adam and Eve). Our sins build a gap between us and God. We become estranged. The worst plight a man can get into is to become estranged in his relationship with one he needs for help. Man had become estranged—separated from God. There was nothing man could do about it. He could not deliver himself.

We need to understand the great estrangement to understand the intervention of God. Man was not only separated but lost. He could not find his way out of the wilderness. He could not understand, in his lostness, the language of God. God always spoke, but man could not understand what He was saying.

To save man, God had to come as man, a servant (Son of Man). Man had sin, and there had to be a withdrawal of Holy God from sinful man. Yet in the punishment, divine love had to reveal itself.

A young boy who disobeyed his father had to be punished. He was sent up in the attic to spend the night. Ten o'clock came, eleven, midnight. He was in the attic, wide-eyed, sleepless, and angry; and there was his father downstairs, also sleepless, thinking about his son. Then it occurred to him that there was something he could do to reveal his love to his son, though he punished him. So he walked up into the attic himself and climbed into bed with his son. He told his son that he had to punish him, but that he had come up to spend the night with him.

Divine love has come to spend the night with us.

Not only has God come to be with us, but to deliver us from our estrangement. He has become not only man, but humiliated man. He has taken our sins upon Himself. Walt Whitman, in his poem "Song of Myself," reflecting on his work among the wounded in the Civil War, wrote, "I do not ask the wounded person how he feels. I myself become the wounded person." Salvation involves love, mercy, forgiveness, restoration. One who is involved in sin cannot forgive and restore. God's only course was to come and put Himself in man's place.

The redemption of man is not simply in the coming of Christ or His becoming servant, teaching, healing, forgiving, but through the cross. He came as a Savior. He died to save—to complete His redemption.

Through redemption, man is restored; he again is in the Father's house where there is joy and peace. The gap has been bridged; he may drift away from God, but there is a bridge from God to man, and he can get back to God in his waywardness. There is an everlasting arm reaching from heaven down to the pit of sin.

So sinful man can sing, "Joy to the world, the Lord is come. Joy to the world, the Savior reigns. Let men their songs employ" (Isaac Watts, from Psalm 98).

> Hark! The herald angels sing,
> Glory to the new-born King;
> Peace on earth, and mercy mild;
> God and sinners reconciled.
>
> Hail the heaven-born Prince of Peace!
> Hail the Son of righteousness!
> Light and life to all He brings,
> Risen with healing in His wings.
> —Charles Wesley

THE SUPREMACY OF LOVE

> All the special gifts and powers from God will come to an end, but love goes on forever. Someday prophecy, and speaking in unknown languages, and special knowledge—these gifts will disappear.
>
> —1 Cor. 13:8 LBV

There are three things that remain—faith, hope, and love—and the greatest of these is love.

First, love is permanent. When all the things in which we glory and pride ourselves have passed away, love will still stand. Waters cannot quench it; neither can the floods drown it.

Love transcends death itself. Love binds the life here on this earth and life beyond this earth, and assures us above knowledge that we shall meet our loved ones again. The pain in our hearts as we stand by the graves of our loved ones causes us to have faith that love is stronger than death.

Second, love is absolute completeness. In this life, we see only the reflections of God. We see that reflection in the gospel, and we see that reflection in Christ. But it is always imperfect and incomplete. But the way of love will lead us to a day in the end when the veil is removed and we shall see face to face. We cannot reach that day without love, because God is love, and only those who love can see God.

Third, love is supreme. It is supreme because of what it can achieve. Love can bring harmony and unity in family life. Members abandon self-interest when love prevails. Love can resolve conflicts between neighbors. Love can bring unity within the church. In our church covenant, we pledge to walk together in Christian love. Walking together in Christian love will result in our exhorting each other unto every good word; to guard each other's reputations, not needlessly exposing the infirmities of others; to participate in each other's joys, and with tender sympathy bear one another's burdens and sorrows; to cultivate Christian courtesy; to be slow to give or take offense, but always ready for reconciliation. Without love, we never achieve unity and harmony within the church.

Love can produce a community—people of diverse backgrounds living together, sharing with one another—concerned about the well-being of one another and working together to enrich the lives of all persons within the neighborhood.

Love can build a nation—persons who love God will seek justice, freedom, brotherhood, and sisterhood, and recognize that God is Father of all persons, and persons are members of His family.

Love can produce world peace. Love wipes out strife, pride, greed, jealousy, self-interest, and hate. Love is the only way to peace between persons and peace between nations. It is supreme because it can achieve what no other gift or virtue can achieve.

Finally, love is supreme because it never ends. It is indestructible. At Calvary, hate and evil nailed love to a cross. But the flag of victory refused to wave over the heads of evil and hateful persons who attempted to put love in the grave. The victory went to love, and it remains with love and will always remain with love.

The future belongs to love. Jesus validated the supremacy of love in His resurrection. Through His resurrection, we can have the assurance that the future belongs to love.

The future does not belong to those who use the power of force, but to those who use the power of love.

> Love looks toward the dawn of the day
> When Jesus shall reign in every nation
> When Jesus shall reign wherever the sun
> Does His successive journeys run,
> His kingdom spread from shore to shore
> Till moons shall wax and wane no more.

People and realms of every tongue
Dwell on His love with sweetest song,
And infant voices shall proclaim
Their early blessings on His name.

—Isaac Watts

Make love your greatest aim so on that day when they crown Jesus Lord of Lords, you can be in that number!

WHAT DOES JESUS MEAN BY "LOVE YOUR NEIGHBOR"?

Eight times in the Bible occurs the commandment: "You shall love your neighbor as yourself" (Mark 12:31 MLB).

Jesus sums up all of the commandments into two. The first and greatest commandment is to love God with all the heart and soul and mind and strength, and the second is like unto it, that you love your neighbor as yourself.

The love of God and the love of neighbor are the two chief commandments in the law, and they stand or fall together.

The Bible makes clear that we cannot love God unless we love our neighbors, and we cannot love and keep loving our neighbor unless we love God.

It should be noted that Jesus said little about the brotherhood of man. He emphasized the fatherhood of God. The assumption is that if we rightly related to God as our Father, we would be brothers and sisters to each other and consequently love and care for one another.

The vision of Jesus was a new kingdom of righteousness, justice, and brotherly and sisterly love upon the earth. In the prayer He taught His disciples to pray, He follows the third petition with: "Give us this day, our daily bread" (Matt. 6:11 KJV). Each of us would seek what we need to be sustained physically not only for ourselves, but for all of God's family. Loving our neighbor would mean that we seek for him or her the same good things that we seek for ourselves.

Perhaps the most striking way in which Jesus speaks of loving your neighbor is in one of His parables, the one commonly called the parable of the Good Samaritan.

What makes a man do what the Good Samaritan did for a stranger, a person of another race? He could have said, "He's a stranger and I have no interest in him, but the decent thing is to stop. Do I pass him by without helping? That would reflect on my reputation, and I must continue to stand well in the community." So for the sake of his own social standing, he lifts the man up.

The Samaritan might have said to himself, "The Bible has laid down the law that we must help others if we are to save our own souls." Jesus in His description of the last judgment declared that those who fail to feed the hungry and help the sick would be cast into darkness. "If I help the poor fellow, I shall have my reward in heaven," the Samartan might have thought. So to insure a star in his crown, he helps the wounded man.

In each case, the motive for helping is self-interest. That falls short of the Good Samaritan's reason.

He had no social standing; he was despised by the injured man. He had not heard of the last judgment with its penalties for failing to help. He was not thinking about saving his soul. He had deep compassion and was concerned about relieving the condition of the beaten man. It was this quality of compassion and love that Jesus was praising.

If we love and care for people, whether friends or strangers, good or bad, poor or rich, white, black, red, we must do what the Samaritan did. Love must have no limits.

MOVING BEYOND THE DREAM

> I hate, I despise your religious feasts; I cannot stand
> your assemblies. Even though you bring me burnt offerings
> and grain offerings, I will not accept them. Though you
> bring choice fellowship offerings, I will have no regard for
> them. Away with the noise of your songs! I will not listen to
> the music of your harps. But let justice roll on like a river,
> righteousness like a never-failing stream!
>
> —Amos 5:21-24 NIV

The call for justice and righteousness by the prophet Amos was
echoed in the "I Have a Dream" speech by the late Martin Luther King
Jr. at the March on Washington.

Sparked by the Rosa Parks incident in Montgomery, Alabama, an
organized movement to eliminate the practice of segregation on public
transportation was launched: a boycott of buses.

The sit-in movement in Greensboro eliminated discrimination at
lunch counters.

In one of the most eloquent and moving speeches ever made, King
called for justice throughout this nation. He visualized a day when
racism, injustice, and inequality, would be abolished, a day when
America would live up to its creed.

To recite the beautiful creed and to sing "America the Beautiful"
amounted to mockery without justice, empty words.

Like the prophet Amos, King recognized that a nation needed
more than having a form of religion and high ideals; it needed to put
them into practice.

Amos declared to religious people: "I hate, I despise your religious
feasts; I cannot stand your assemblies. Even though you bring me burnt
offerings and grain offerings, I will not accept them. Though you bring

choice fellowship offerings, I will have no regard for them. Away with the noise of your songs! I will not listen to the music of your harps. But let justice roll on like a river, righteousness like a never-failing stream."

King's dream was that one day enough people in enough places in America would rise up and make justice, equality, and the dignity of personhood more than ideals. This was what a Christian nation ought to achieve. This was what the God of all nations would will for America, which had been blessed.

Since the national holiday observance honoring King, the theme has been "Keeping King's Dream Alive." The nation cannot permit a noble dream like that to die—especially a nation that emphasizes "one nation under God with liberty and justice for all."

Keeping the dream alive has been important and is important, but is not sufficient. What America needs to do, and what we, as a minority race, need to do is to move beyond the dream. Noble dreams are of no real value unless they become more than dreams. Dreams and ideals are valuable only as they take wings and become reality.

The greatest thing we can do to honor the selfless and noble life of Martin Luther King is to put legs and arms on the high ideals he dreamed of: to work to abolish racism. Racism is still real in America. Unemployment rates are always higher among blacks. Blacks are twice as likely to be unemployed as whites. Many become discouraged because of economic distress, poverty and hopelessness.

King was not only a symbol of love, nonviolence, and hope, but a proponent of economic justice. It doesn't mean much to have free access to lunch counters without money to pay for the lunch. We have not obtained real equality as a race. When we have moved to contend for economic justice, whites walked away with the excuse that it cost too much—education, job creation and training, decent housing, health care for all. They don't want to be taxed more. Economic justice is not perceived as righteous.

The cry of Amos: "Let justice and righteousness flood the land."

King: "Righteousness leads to justice." Do the right thing. Move beyond the dream.

Challenge in a small and seemingly insignificant way. Support efforts and groups designed to bring about justice, such as the NAACP.

Vote for candidates who have shown interest in problems of the poor. Call for and take advantage of job training programs. Encourage others to do so.

King is a symbol of love and hope. Love the downtrodden. Give hope to the hopeless.

King followed the example of selflessness. His father pleaded with him not to go to Memphis. He counted not his life dear to himself that he might lift Godward, upward, his brothers and sisters.

Move to fulfill the dream of Amos and King.

PEACE, A GIFT FROM GOD

I will lift up mine eyes unto the hills, from whence
cometh my help.

—Ps. 121:1 KJV

A Methodist minister, several years ago, had an article in *Pulpit Digest* in which he said, "If we will look away from ourselves and look toward God, we will find the help we so badly need for our lives."

Several psychiatrists have labeled our age as neurotic. They cite the increase in ailments caused by tension and emotional distress as evidence. People today have more time to relax (with a forty-hour week), and long vacation periods (at least some people do), which should make us happier and healthier, but the grim fact is that we are not as happy as our fathers and mothers. We live longer than they did, but we are nervous, fearful, hard—pressed, easily upset, easily irritated, have little energy, and have little zeal.

With all of the advancement in medical science, we have not been healed of diseases resulting from unwholesome tensions. A physician in the sixties observed and concluded that we don't have nervous systems to keep pace with modern civilization.

He advised that failure to manage tension is a major health problem and recommended three steps.

First, look inside yourself.

Understand what fear, anger, worry, and hate do to the glands and organs. Realize that these emotions upset the entire system and lead to nervous breakdowns, to heart and kidney failures when too frequently indulged in.

Second, look at yourself.

Look inside yourself and then look at yourself. His reasoning is that we rush and worry needlessly. If we could see ourselves as others see us, simple pride would stop us. When we are angry and lose control, we should look in the mirror. We would see how ugly we can be with frowns, our jaws clenched.

Third, he said, we need to look away from ourselves.

Practice lifting your mind above the rush and confusion around us. Take time throughout the day to think of something pleasant, something uplifting.

We must be willing to let medical personnel look inside us—examine our organs—but there is something our faith wants to say concerning looking away from ourselves. The psalmist says, in his confusion and helplessness, "I will lift up mine eyes unto the hills, from whence cometh my help." It's the one place help can always come from.

In Psalm 19, the psalmist bids us to look away from ourselves that we may see the glory of God, the maker of all things, and rejoice in His majesty, His loving care, and boundless mercy toward us.

Look up and see a loving and compassionate Father who understands our weakness and forgives our sins. In the conclusion of Psalm 19, we have words that have been put in very personal terms: "Let the words of my mouth and the meditation of my heart be acceptable in Thy sight, O Lord, my Rock and my Redeemer" (Ps. 19:14 RSV).

We have in these words the heart of our faith and devotion: an awareness of God, an awareness of our dependence upon Him. The psalmist—a person confused, upset with the ways of God; like us, tensed over the things which were happening that he had no control over—honestly looked away from himself and looked toward God, and then wisely looked again at himself.

To find the help we need in this neurotic age in which we live, we must look away from ourselves and look toward God.

The deep longings of our souls can be supplied only by our maker.

We try in vain to find the power within us even to live a decent life. Wretched and helpless in our strivings, we cry, is there a way to be a decent person? We long for a life of contentment in a changing world. How can we hold to sacred values in a world that labels them outdated? We don't always feel comfortable when we are not in tune with what is happening around us. We are prone to be conformist—even when deep inside we don't feel comfortable conforming.

I met an elderly lady the other week in a drugstore. She was embarrassed for me to see her dressed like a 16-year-old. She dropped her head in shame and apologized. "I didn't have time to change and get here before the drugstore closed," she said. "I'm so sorry you caught me like this."

Typical in this day—the world is too much with us, and the values of yesterday have been pushed aside to conform to values that shame us deep down.

In this world of change, we must be careful to hold on to those values and moral principles that ought not to be pushed aside.

Be faithful to the teachings of One who does not change and whose teachings are valid eternally. He is not only the same as yesterday, but what He taught is valid.

One thing that all of us deeply long for in this restless, confused, tense world is peace. There is an insanity growing all around us, and we live in fear that some mentally sick person will have a shooting spree while we are shopping in some store or at a bank. It is extremely difficult to be at ease and feel secure anywhere today. A bombing in New York and planned bombing beyond frighten us.

The sale of sleeping pills has doubled in the past ten years. The pressures of our day in work, in home life, in just living, make it impossible for persons to relax and get a peaceful rest.

The kind of peace that we so badly desire and long for cannot be achieved by us. It is a gift of God. We must look and pray to God, for Jesus said to troubled disciples before His crucifixion, "Let not your heart be troubled." Don't be upset! "Believe in God, believe also in Me" (John 14:1 KJV). Later on, He said to them: "My peace I give unto you; not as the world giveth" (John 14:27 KJV).

That peace quiets our souls when the storms rage in our lives and they are not calmed. I have come to know that peace in the midst of conflict and criticism. Storms rage on the outside and calmness prevails on the inside. It is well with my soul. Whatever my lot, with the God of peace, it is well!

IMITATING CHRIST

As Jesus was walking beside the Sea of Galilee, he saw two brothers, Simon called Peter, and his brother Andrew. They were casting a net into the lake, for they were fishermen. "Come, follow me," Jesus said, "and I will make you fishers of men." At once they left their nets and followed him.

—Matt. 4:18-20 NIV

A Christian is one who tries to follow Christ. "Follow me" appears at the beginning of the Gospel. After Christ had spent forty days in the wilderness being tempted by the devil, he came forth preaching, "Repent: for the kingdom of heaven is at hand" (Matt. 4:17 RSV). He began thereafter His recruiting campaign for disciples.

As a recruiting commander, He simply said to those He wanted to enlist, "Follow me!" To follow required those who enlisted not only to surrender their lives, but to imitate Christ.

Five hundred fifty years ago, *The Imitation of Christ* appeared and became one of the influential books next to the Bible. The opening line of the book has a quotation from Christ, as found in John 8:12 RSV: "He who follows me will not walk in darkness."

The words of Christ call on followers to imitate His life and example. We need to pattern our lives after Him to achieve discipline. One of the great struggles of life is that of discipline. How can life be brought under control when it threatens to defeat our choice, dreams, and ambitions?

Those early disciples of Jesus discovered that the secret of His life of discipline was His prayer life. It was the key to the tremendous power He had. The desperate need for those of us who call ourselves Christians is to imitate Christ in His prayer life.

Prayer is the heart of vital religion. Prayer in the life of Christ was a constant communing with the heavenly Father. It was an experience of pure trust and loving obedience to the Father. He prayed as naturally as a child breathes. He prayed alone in the garden, on the mountain, beside the sea, in the wilderness, in the temple. He also prayed in the presence of others, essentially a communing with God. We are not as close to the Father as Christ was, but we can commune with the same Father. The same Father provides power for us to overcome our temptations.

NEVERTHELESS

The word *nevertheless* has always made history. It is the conjunction that introduces an exception or a qualification. It points out that there are two sides to a question.

The apostle Paul uses the word in speaking of his suffering as a result of the gospel. "For this gospel I was appointed a preacher and apostle and teacher, and therefore I suffer as I do. But I am not ashamed, for I know whom I have believed, and I am sure that he is able to guard until that day what has been entrusted to me" (2 Tim. 1:11-12 RSV).

There was suffering on one hand, but on the other was uncrushable hope. Against his frustration was faith in the sustaining power of God.

Jesus uses the conjunction when speaking of the death of Lazarus. "Lazarus is dead. And I am glad for your sakes that I was not there, to the intent ye may believe; nevertheless let us go to him" (John 11:14-15 KJV).

Again Jesus uses the word in His prayer on the Mount of Olives. "When He came to the place He said to them, 'Pray that you may not enter into temptation.' And He withdrew from them about a stone's throw, and knelt down and prayed, 'Father, if thou art willing, remove this cup from me; nevertheless not my will, but Thine, be done'" (Luke 22:40-42 RSV).

Nevertheless always confronts us in prayer. There is always our side and God's side. The great struggle in prayer is the struggle we face daily in life. What do we want versus what does God want for us? Our will versus God's will.

In His struggle in the Garden of Gethsemane, Jesus, after considering His side against God's side, offers seven words that became the greatest words, the greatest prayer, ever prayed: "not my will, but Thine be done."

He dreaded the cup; nevertheless, He recognized that God's purposes should prevail.

In anguish, Jesus said, "Now is my soul troubled" (John 12:27 KJV) as he begins His prayer in the garden. He was distressed and troubled. His agony was revealed to the three disciples with Him. He prayed again and again in the garden that the hour might pass from Him. He did not want to die, and He prayed until sweat became like great drops of blood falling down upon the ground.

Nevertheless, He could not lose sight of the fact that life was for glorifying God. He had taught His disciples to pray "Thy will be done" and "Thine is the kingdom and the glory." Christ would have His disciples understand that God's will must prevail if God is to be glorified. Although there are two sides to a question, mature persons always end up cooperating with God.

Suffering is not what we want. Nevertheless, we believe that in the long run it will be best for His work.

Christ's opening Sermon on the Mount assures disciples.

> Blessed [happy] are the poor in spirit for theirs is the kingdom of God. Blessed [happy] are those who mourn for they shall be comforted . . . Blessed [happy] are those who are persecuted because of righteousness, for theirs is the kingdom of heaven. Blessed [happy] are you when people insult you, persecute you and falsely say all kinds of evil against you because of me. Rejoice and be glad, because great is your reward in heaven.
>
> —Matt. 5:3-4, 10-12 NIV

Happy moments in life are the moments when we crucify self and say *nevertheless*. Great times are times when we look at our side and God's side and say, "Thy will, Lord, be done."

The way is rough and rocky, Nevertheless, I must be on my way. The adversaries are frightening. Nevertheless, I must be on my way.

The valley appears too deep for me to tread. Nevertheless, I must be on my way. The journey seems endless. Nevertheless, I must be on my way. I must go ahead to my Calvary because only at Calvary can I give myself away.

Here, Lord, I give myself away.
'Tis all that I can do.
At the cross, at the cross where I first saw the light,
And the burden of my heart rolled away,
It was there by faith
I received my sight,
And now I am happy all the day.

—Isaac Watts

PASSING THE BREAD AROUND

The great prayer for mankind is the prayer that Jesus taught His disciples to pray. Before He offers the prayer, the master teacher emphasized: "This, then, is how you should pray" (Matt. 6:9 NIV).

In the prayer, which millions recite daily, is a summary of all of the teachings of our Lord.

Our Father: God is the Father of all mankind. Mankind is designed as a family.

Hallowed be thy name: God is holy.

Thy kingdom come: the only system that is abiding is God's system. Kingdoms built by men are transient, defective. Only God can bring into being a perfect and enduring kingdom.

Thy will be done: we are here to do God's will. The kingdom of God can come only as He reigns. The greatest moment—the greatest achievement—is doing His will.

Fourth petition: the first means to be fulfilled for the coming of the kingdom is that His will must be done.

The second means is that bread must be passed around.

The first request for mankind is that bread would be supplied. "Give us today our daily bread" (Matt. 6:11 NIV). God is concerned about our frail and feeble physical bodies. These bodies need to be preserved in order to give our minds and spirit a chance.

Jesus in His teachings and ministry gave considerable emphasis to the physical well-being of persons.

As He began His public ministry, He stood up and read from the book of the prophet Isaiah: "The Spirit of the Lord is upon me, because he hath anointed me to preach the gospel to the poor; because He has sent me to heal the broken hearted, to preach deliverance to the captives, and recovering of sight to the blind, to set at liberty them that are bruised" (Luke 4:18 KJV).

As the Master went about, He revealed the concern of His Father about physical suffering. He healed the hungry. Though He warned about men living by bread alone, He emphasized the necessity of bread. Without bread, men sicken and die.

It is because of the concern of the heavenly Father that men should have bread that Jesus bids us pray, "Give us this day our daily bread."

One of the basic problems in our world is that of bread. Much of the unrest and strife result today from hunger.

Hungry people cannot understand why a nation must give priority to building and maintaining military power.

Dying in poverty, people cannot understand how a nation can spend more destroying human life abroad that it can on saving human life at home.

What does it profit a nation to destroy its people in an attempt to maintain security?

What the great teacher would have us understand when we pray this fourth petition is that it is a request that God would help us pass the bread around so that the billions who are starving in our world can be fed.

The prayer itself seeks to create an awareness that mankind is a family. We are our brother's keeper because we are our brother's brother. Brothers care! Brothers share!

We are taught to pray "give us" in order that we can recognize that it is God's will that the entire family will be provided adequate food, sufficient clothes, decent homes, medical care, and the opportunity to develop the mind.

When we pray the prayer, we are asking God to supply the needs of our brothers through us. Help us to use our minds, our energies, and the other resources He provides us to bless others.

There is a very striking statement in the story of the man with two sons: the hired servants had food enough and to spare.

We must care enough about our brothers to share.

LORD, TO WHOM CAN WE GO?

Many are turning away from Christ in our age and following new religious leaders. Some are joining established religions that are seeking to extend their horizons.

The claim of most of those drifters is that they seek something they can understand. They argue that it is extremely difficult to understand the teachings of Jesus and to comply with the great moral demands imposed upon them by His religion. They want something simple, less demanding.

After Jesus had fed the five thousand on a mountain across from Lake Galilee and walked back across the lake to the other side, He began teaching the crowd still trailing behind Him. The great teacher speaks of Himself as the bread of life, the bread that came down from heaven, a kind of bread that kills hunger forever.

What the Master was attempting to get them to understand was that He was flesh and blood. It was essential for men to accept the fact that Jesus was both divine and human. God had taken human life upon Himself and had come to be like men so that men could become like Him.

In Jesus, we see God taking on the form of humanity so that He could face our human situation—struggling with our problems, battling with our temptations, suffering our hurts.

It is important that we understand the manhood of our Lord so that when we are discouraged and in despair, when we are tired of life and beaten to our knees and disgusted, when we are lonely and sick, we know that Jesus understands and has taken life's struggles on Himself. He knows our weakness; He knows our heartaches. He knows our every need. We can relate to Him.

Jesus said to those followers, "For my flesh is real food and my blood is real drink. Whoever eats my flesh and drinks my blood remains in me, and I in him" (John 6:55-56 NIV). To eat Christ's body is to feed on the thought of His manhood until our manhood is strengthened and cleansed and purified by His. To drink His blood is to take into our veins new life and vitality.

What Jesus is saying is that He must be more than a symbol. So long as He is a symbol, He is outside of men. He needs to enter into the hearts of men. As with a book on the shelf (outside), we have to take it off the shelf and read it for it to become a part of us. We must take His life inside if we are to have life, real life.

That is clearly what the Master meant when he speaks of Himself as the vine. "I am the vine . . . If a man remains in me and I in him, he will bear much fruit; apart from me you can do nothing" (John 15:5 NIV). If life is to be revitalized, then the bread of life and the blood of life must permeate and saturate our lives.

The crowd following Him found His teachings hard to understand, hard to accept, hard to tolerate. They knew that He was from God and that He offered the hope of eternity, but they were not willing to accept the moral demands He would impose upon them, so they left Him.

"You do not want to leave too, do you?" Jesus asked the Twelve.

Simon Peter answered, "Lord, to whom shall we go? You have the words of eternal life" (John 6:67-68 NIV).

To whom can we go? Who else can offer us what you can? No one! It's foolish to leave and go where you will be worse off. It's senseless to leave unless we know we are going to better ourselves. We ought not to give up the greatest for the great. Change ought always to improve things.

Nobody can do for us what Christ can do. People who walk away from Christ to become followers of other religious leaders and movements receive the short end of the bargain. No one can teach us about life as Christ can. He is God and yet man.

Other religious leaders and movements claim to be the way to the good life, but only Christ can say, "I am the bread of life; I am the blood of life."

Other religious leaders can teach truth, but only Christ can say, "I am truth." "Then you will know the truth, and the truth will set you free" (John 8:32 NIV).

Christ is still our leader. He is hailed today as the bread of life, the living water. He is proclaimed as the light of the world, the Comforter, the Great Physician, the Good Shepherd, the lily of the valley, the rose of Sharon, the bridge over deep water.

Other star leaders have disappeared from the platform, but Christ is looked to as the bright morning star.

Other kings have taken their orbit into space, but the King of Kings is still commanding the winds to be still and the storms to cease.

Others who come on the scene and set up their little kingdoms are remembered by their teachings, but the Lord of the universe is still among us.

Others have come and gone and they have not come back, but the man who was crucified on a Friday is saying: all power has been given to me. We still sing

> How sweet the name of Jesus sounds
> In a believer's ear!
> It soothes his sorrows, heals his wounds,
> And drives away his fear.
>
> It makes the wounded spirit whole,
> And calms the troubled breast.
> 'Tis manna to the hungry soul
> And to the weary rest.
>
> —John Newton

REMEMBER

But thou shalt remember the Lord thy God: for it is he
that giveth thee power to get wealth.

—Deut. 8:18 KJV

This is one of the strongest, most powerful, and most needed passages in the Bible dealing with the problem of mankind and womankind.

The text is directed to the people of Israel but speaks to every nation, every race, and every person.

The Israelites had completed their long and rough journey from Egypt to the Promised Land. They had been in slavery under Pharaoh, and the Lord had brought them out of Egypt with a mighty hand. For forty years, they had traveled through the terrible and frightening wilderness with its fiery serpents, even across the Red Sea, and the dry ground. God had sustained them and protected them from seen and unseen dangers.

They had reached the point where the Promised Land could be seen. They could see that it was a good land, a land of brooks, of fountains, and springs in the valleys and springs in the mountains. It was a land of wheat, barley, and vines and fig trees and a land of olive oil and honey—a dreamland.

Just before they moved into that dreamland, they were told to remember the Lord, for it was He who gave them power. It was the Lord who had given them the good land. Therefore, they were told to remember Him.

The warning to the power of Israel to remember the One who gives power is a vital and an extremely important and needed message for the nations today and for every person on the face of this earth: remember.

This is a day when we marvel at the power of nations. Nations have put together weapons that can blow up other nations in a twinkle of the eye. They have been able to built spaceships that can circle outer space and land on the moon. They have put together a communication system that enables nations to communicate with nations around the world in a matter of minutes. We can look at a tube and see what is happening throughout this vast universe.

Viewing the achievements of nations and persons of this day of scientific and technical advancement, we are prone to sing, "Glory to men and women in the highest" instead of "Glory to God in the highest."

In this age, when we are blessed with good homes, the best food to eat, healthy bodies and minds, a few CDs, mutual funds, enough money to send our kids to college, graduate and professional schools, we forget the source of our blessings. We fail to remember from whom all of our blessings flow.

The people of Israel, in their prosperity, were warned to remember that it was God who gave them power to prosper and to become what they were. They did not generate that power. It was a gift from God—a gracious and kind God. They did not deserve such blessings. They were gifts from a merciful God.

One of the worst things that can happen to a nation and to a race of people is to forget who gives power. A rich famer with great possessions may forget the source of blessings and become greedy and self-centered. He might think that he produced goods on his own, forgetting that he didn't create the land; he did not create the seed; he had nothing to do with the rain; he certainly didn't cause the sun to come out.

Any person who fails to remember the source from whom blessings come is a fool. When we fail to remember the One who gives us power and to thank Him, we become fools (not only ignorant, but foolish).

An insane person in a nursing home asked the nurse if she had thanked God that morning. The nurse replied, "For what?" Patient replied, "For sanity."

Every day that we live, we ought to remember what the Lord has done and is doing for us. Every moment, He is blessing us.

Thank God for the great things He does for you and thank Him for what you sometimes think of as little things.

Thank Him for the air we breathe.

Thank Him for the sunshine that warms our bodies and the sunshine that warms our spirits.

Thank Him for eyes to see, ears to hear, tongues to speak, and hands to work.

Thank Him for the water you drink and for the food you eat.

Thank Him when you get up in the morning. Remember that it was He who touched you with the finger of love and woke you up.

Remember when you sit down at the breakfast table that the food you eat comes from the hand of God.

Remember when you go out of the house and breathe fresh air that God provides.

Remember, when you get into your car, that God provided the materials to build your car, the knowledge and skill of men to put it together, and even the gas to run it.

Remember that the energy you have to move is given by God.

Remember, when you return safely home, that it was God's hand that guided you over the dangerous roads you traveled.

Remember, when you get your paycheck, that God provided you with the strength to work and the door for employment.

Always remember that the earth is the Lord's and the fullness thereof. This is God's world and is maintained by His mighty hand. Without Him, this world would cave in.

Remember that if you succeed in life, it is God who gives you power!

Celebrate Him for His goodness every day.

Praise Him for His loving kindness.

Praise Him for His mercy.

Praise Him for Jesus whom He sent to save us!

UNFAILING SUPPORTING ARMS

> The eternal God is your dwelling place, and underneath
> are the everlasting arms.
>
> —Deut. 33:27 MLB

We will never outgrow our need for support. A sense of security in this world of ever-present danger is achieved only through realizing that underneath are undergirding arms—arms that support us and aid us in life's floods that threaten to wash us away.

The Bible speaks of God's providence in glowing terms. But perhaps no passage sums up God's love and care as well as our text: "The eternal God is your dwelling place, and underneath are the everlasting arms."

Israel dwelt in safety, not because of her strength, but because underneath were mighty arms.

When we speak of the providence of God, our minds first reflect on special acts and events that we call providential. From auto accidents survived to impossible escapes, we are convinced that a power beyond us intervened in our behalf, such as you miss a flight and the plane you were to catch goes down. The Bible tells us how the children of Israel escaped.

After the children of Israel had safely crossed the Red Sea and pursuing Egyptians were engulfed in the waters, the Israelites were convinced it was an act of divine deliverance, the undergirding hands of God. The book of Exodus records the song of Moses and his people praising God for the greatness of His arm.

All of us can recall events when we know that God intervened in our behalf.

However, Jesus warns us about interpreting misfortunes as always being marks of God's disfavor. Likewise, all fortunate escapes and successes are not signs of God's special liking. Life is always too complex for neat explanations.

Nevertheless, blessings do burst upon us in unexpected ways. When they come, we should be humbly grateful to God for undeserved mercy. This should lead to deeper dedication.

While we do feel the presence of God's undergirding, of supporting arms in special events, it is more satisfactory to look for God's providence in the natural order of events.

A higher understanding of God's providence is presented in the story of Job—a devout and upright man, yet afflicted with loss of property, loss of sons and daughters, and loss of health. Finally at the bottom of the valley, Job heard a voice out of the whirlwind asking, "Hast thou an arm like God?" (Job 40:9 KJV).

The voice had mentioned some of the mighty things wrought by the arm of the Lord.

"Where were you when I laid the foundations of the earth"? . . . "Or who shut in the sea with doors . . ." " . . . or who has begotten the drops of dew? . . ." "From whose womb did the ice come forth? . . ." "Can you send forth lightnings . . ." "Who has put wisdom in the clouds . . ." (Job 38:4, 8, 28-29, 35-36 RSV).

A higher understanding of God's care leads us to look into the sky and say with the psalmist, "The heavens declare the glory of God; and the firmament sheweth his handywork" (Ps. 19:1 KJV).

But what about the bad things in nature? Wild beasts in the jungle. Weeds that choke out the flowers. Tornadoes that destroy towns.

One explanation is that the bad things help life to be good. How could there be courage if there were no dangers? How could there be love if there were no misunderstanding?

Like Job, we cannot understand all the mysteries of this vast universe. We do not fully understand what many things are or why they are.

WHAT ARE WE LOOKING FOR?

The whole history of man is the story of his long search for salvation. Everyone, in some way, is looking for salvation—soldiers, statesmen, poets and prophets, socialists and communists, kings and common men.

There are two kinds of people in the world. If you trace the long history of man's search for salvation, you will find these two elements and these two kinds of people: those who think of salvation mainly as a magical process that does something for us, and those who think of it as a power that does something in us.

Christ came to a people looking with earnest expectation for a deliverer, mostly a deliverer who would give them something, do something for them, and change their intolerable conditions. They wanted a military messiah who would lead the revolution against Rome and give them back their lost kingdom.

That hope, which in the minds of the prophets had meant an inner, spiritual redemption, had been twisted by bitter conditions into a political, materialistic hope. They had come to think of deliverance not from the evil in themselves but from the evil in their enemies; they wanted to be saved from that.

Jesus in His ministry had to choose between the material salvation that the people wanted and the deeper salvation that they needed; He had to make up His mind whether He would be a savior doing something for them or be a savior doing something in them.

He was concerned about poverty and bread, yet he realized that the bread problem is everlastingly rooted in the spiritual and that it can be solved only by getting certain ideas and evils out of people's hearts. If we learned the words *love, brotherhood,* and *justice,* the bread problem could be solved. No man on this earth would go hungry if we understood these other words from the mouth of God.

Seeing that what He did for them must be something done within them, Jesus rejected the materialistic philosophy that has brought the modern world to suicidal strife.

He rejected too the appeal to magic. People will follow anybody who will do tricks for them or will get things done for them by miracle so that they won't have to do those things themselves. He knew that magic doesn't make people good, that doing things for people doesn't change their hearts, doesn't get the evil out. It often puts evil in. It encourages people to look to God to do for them what He must do within them if they are to be His sons.

"And thou shalt call his name Jesus; for he shall save his people from their sins" (Matt. 1:21 KJV). God breaks into human life to do something for man that man could not do for himself. The gospel is to save people, change them, make them something, cure the evil in their hearts, and make them different.

Christianity has come to be little more than a craving for protection, a device to insure safety from hell and the punishment of sin without saving from the sin.

A medal, blessed in the name of Christ, becomes a charm of protection on the highway or the battlefield.

Salvation by formula: a man wanting to be saved and go to heaven is instructed to believe in a set of doctrines; then he has something he is told is salvation.

What must I do to be saved? versus What must I do to be safe?

There are always people who want to feel good without being good. We need Christ to save us from very definite sin, to cure us of stinginess, fear, selfishness, bad temper, and all that is wrong in us, which together makes all the trouble in God's world.

Christ was rejected by His people, and the world rejects Him still because His ideas of salvation are deeper and more inward than we care to go.

If we want a brotherly world, we must be brothers. If we want to get the evils out of our relationships, we must get the evils out of ourselves. If we want a new spirit in the world, we must be born of His Spirit in our hearts. He is the Savior. He is the great light shining in our dark!

GOD AND OUR TIME

> We must work the works of Him who sent me, while it
> is day; night comes, when no one can work.
>
> —John 9:4 RSV

Our time, like our talents, and our money, is a gift from God. God entrusts us with time. It is not ours to do with as we please.

A good steward does not waste his master's money. Neither does a good steward waste the time his master entrusts to him. Time is precious.

A time killer is never a good steward. He is wasting time that really belongs to somebody else. The person who sits around loafing one day out of a week in seventy years will have wasted four-and-a-half years of God's time.

The slothful person robs God and others of time. The slothful leader who runs ten minutes late for a meeting will not simply delay the meeting for ten minutes, but will rob ten persons on time of one hour and forty minutes.

The sleeper who sleeps too much is not a good steward.

The person who tries to do alone what cannot be done alone is robbing God of His time. Some things cannot be done alone; we need to work with others to get some things done.

God holds us responsible for all our time. We must account as stewards for the time we have wasted when we should have been working the works of Him who has given us time.

In the text, Jesus is saying that the hours of life are few and limited, and there is a task for every hour.

First, He would have us get a sense of purpose. We must work the works of Him who sent us.

The One who speaks was one who made the best use of time. There was no standing still in idleness, no wandering around in circles in His life. He had a sense of purpose.

We are sent to do a work for God. We are on an errand for God, with something important to deliver. We must not throw away precious time. We must work while the opportunity remains.

Second, Jesus is saying that we must have a sense of urgency about our work for God.

We are limited. Time is controlled by someone else. We must work while it is day. While there is breath in our bodies, we must get the job done.

Tomorrow is never a time to get things done. That's why gradualism is a terrible thing. To put off something that we ought to do today expresses an attitude that we control time.

God controls time, and the only time we have to get things done is today. Get your work done today.

Christ has entrusted the work to our hands. He has sent us. "As my Father hath sent me, even so send I you" (John 20:21 KJV). The only way that we can get His work done is while life is in our bodies.

For the night will come when no man can work. Peace comes only when we have done our work, miserable death when we have not finished our work. Jesus calls us today. Work in the vineyard. Get right with God.

PUTTING IT ALL TOGETHER FOR THE GLORY OF GOD

From Sunday, September 5, through Sunday, October 3, the pastor has been preaching on "Putting It All Together for the Glory of God."

The series of sermons has been designed to make members of Shiloh more clearly understand that the church is not a building but God's people united in fellowship to work for Him.

In our first sermon, "Putting Together a Vital Prayer Life," we stressed the necessity of the people of God being in constant communion with Him. We cannot feel His power and discover His will unless we are plugged into Him. Consequently, the church must come together to cultivate a vital life with God through prayer and worship.

Not only must there be prayer and worship, but there must be real fellowship among the people of God. Our second sermon dealt with "Putting Together Real Fellowship within the Church." Love for God always leads to love for our fellow creatures. We expressed the aspiration that Shiloh would not be known primarily for the beautiful building that will be erected but for the quality of love for God and earthly companions. It would be great if we cultivate a love within the church that would cause non-Christians to say of us as was said of the early church: "See how these Christians love one another."

The most important thing is not to find the correct creed, the form of government, a structure that is designed to look like a church, but for those within the church to act like a church, loving one another through caring and sharing.

Our third sermon was titled "Putting Together an Outreach Program." As we emphasize each Sunday, the church building and the fellowship are not ends but means to ends. We must not only heed the Master's command to come but also His command to go. The church is to be God's servant in offering light to those who live in darkness. Light is useless unless it penetrates the darkness.

Let us not be like the prophet Jonah, trying to escape the call to go to the modern Ninevehs to proclaim God's love and mercy. God's love is not limited to those with the church fellowship. The good news is that "For God loved the world so much that He gave His only Son, so that anyone who believes in him shall not perish" (John 3:16 LBV).

In keeping with our groundbreaking for the new church building, our fourth sermon in the series dealt with "Putting the Building Together." We warned against making the building a god. Rather, it should be a place where the <u>living</u> God is worshipped. Nothing put together by men deserves worshiping. Only Him who has made us is entitled to be worshiped. We must strive to let the church building be an equipping station for God's people—a place where we come to better equip ourselves to go forth and be God's servants.

Our final sermon is centered around Christian stewardship, emphasizing that the church cannot provide the type of ministries so badly needed in our day unless we as church members recognize that we are stewards. The apostle Paul reminds us, "You are not your own" (1 Cor. 6:19 RSV).

The church, as the people of God, must constantly be reminded that we were "bought with a price."

> The Church's one foundation
> Is Jesus Christ her Lord;
> She is His new creation,
> By water and the Word;
> From heaven He came and sought her
> To be His holy bride.
> With His own blood he bought her
> And for her life He died.
>   —Samuel J. Stone

Recognizing that we are stewards, we must not act as if time is ours to be used as we please. Our talents are entrusted to us by God to be used to glorify Him through blessing others. Gold and silver are not creations of men. Men discovered them. Our money cannot be used as we please if we recognize our stewardship. It is used to please God. We don't do with our lives what we please, but strive to please God.

For the church to do what Christ established it to do, we must be Christian stewards. We must be businesslike in supporting the kingdom of God. Whenever we receive income (salaries, retirement checks), we must religiously first put aside a portion for God. He owns all of it, but asks us for only one tenth. A portion of our time must be religiously used each day to help others and make the church more effective. We must never refuse to use our talents to strengthen the church and bless others.

Let us put it all together for the glory of God!

ALIVE OUTSIDE BUT DEAD INSIDE

Jesus Christ, the once dead but living Lord, reveals to John the Revelator messages to the seven churches of Asia Minor.

Asia Minor was one of the first places in the world to become civilized. The Hittite kingdom developed there nineteen hundred years before Christ.

Seven churches were established in the seven major cities of Asia Minor. The churches all confronted pagan religions and persecution.

Many members of the churches became more loyal to emperors than to Christ. Some worshiped emperors rather than God. John was exiled for refusing to deny Christ and worship emperors as divine. It is through a faithful follower that the risen Christ speaks to the seven churches. The Word is through John, but not from John.

To Smyrna: "This message is from Him who is the First and Last, who was dead and then came back to life" (Rev. 2:8 LBV).

To Laodicea: "This message is from the one who stands firm, the faithful and true witness" (Rev. 3:14 LBV).

The messages to the seven contain words of encouragement but also words of judgment. Only to Laodicea did the risen Christ give words of judgment alone. He had nothing good to say about the church, which lost completely its sense of meaning, its purpose for being.

One message was to the church of Sardis. It had the reputation of being alive but was dead.

Everything that appears to be living is not alive. In our day, we have specialized in making the unreal look real—teeth, hair, face, flowers, trees, fruit.

The church at Sardis looked like a church that was really alive. It was a flourishing church. It had standing. It had wealth. It was outwardly alive, but inwardly it was decaying.

There can be a decay in religion even while religion grows. We have seen a growth in religion in the twentieth century and at the same time a decay in religion. There is a form of godliness, but no power. Paul pointed to men "having a form of godliness but denying its power" (2 Tim. 3:5 NIV). Outside Sardis was alive, but inside it was dead.

When does a church decay or die? When it begins to worship its own past. Whenever it lives on its memories and fails to find new challenges. Water becomes stagnant when it stops flowing.

The church that is not moving forward is moving backward. A church dies when it worships its own past, when it is more concerned with forms than with life. We can become so hung up on how things are done that we don't get them done. Procedures can be curses as well as blessings. Forms ought not to reduce the effectiveness of the church. Procedures ought not to keep the church from getting the job done.

Creeds are no good without deeds.

A church dies when the material is worshiped. God only is to be worshiped. God is not wood. God is not brick. He is not form. He is spirit. Not only the church but man dies when he resorts to worshiping that which is lower than he is.

A church dies when Christ is not lifted up. The warning of the risen Christ to Sardis: "Be watchful, and strengthen the things which remain" (Rev. 3:2 KJV). First, be watchful at our weakest point, and second, the church needs to be watchful at our strongest point. Sardis failed to be watchful. It is dangerous to say, "This or that I will never do."

CHEER THE WEARY TRAVELER!

The Lord God hath given me the tongue of the learned,
that I should know how to speak a word in season to him
that is weary.

—Isa. 50:4 KJV

We who are strong ought to bear with the failings of the
weak, and not to please ourselves.

—Rom. 15:1 RSV

Black slave songs express the thoughts, hopes, and emotions of slaves. The slave preacher dealt with the problems of liberation, consolations, and weariness of slaves in his preaching. In their secret camp meetings, they were lifted from hopelessness to uncrushable hope.

They came to camp meetings often crushed in spirit because of cruel treatment, discouraged because of mounting tribulations, weary of waiting for liberation, but they left with new power gushing up within their souls. Religion gave them strength and courage to stand up under affliction and in despair.

Religion also gave them concern for their fellow slaves; many were not able to get to the camp meetings.

Their love and concern for those slaves are expressed in several slave songs. Among them is "Cheer the Weary Traveler." Love was not only on the lips of the slaves; it was in their hearts.

From the camp meetings, slaves would go forth to "cheer the weary traveler." They carried out the words in Romans: "We who are strong ought to bear with the failings of the weak, and not to please ourselves." They put it in these words:

Don't be weary, traveler.
Come along home to Jesus;
Don't be weary, traveler.
Come along home to Jesus.

This song expresses a quality of soul and a real understanding of how to handle weariness.

They showed a concern for others who were traveling that rough road. Many were getting weary of the journey. They wanted to lay down the heavy load. The stronger ones tried to help the weak slaves to carry their heavy loads, to face tribulation and despair. "Don't be weary, traveler," they would sing. "Come along home to Jesus. My head got wet with the midnight dew. Come along home to Jesus. Angels bear me witness, too. Come along home to Jesus."

Their religion was characterized by the spirit of sharing their faith. Faith dies when it is not shared.

The song not only reflects the quality of soul of the slaves, but also their insight and understanding.

It is not only a plea for them not to be weary, but it tells them where to go when weariness is a burden.

So often we plead with people not to be discouraged—don't be weary; don't be this and that—without telling them where to go when their burdens get them down.

Slaves pleaded with fellow travelers, "Don't be weary, traveler," and then told them where to go for the answer. Come along home to Jesus. This is where it's at.

Jesus gives the invitation to the weary: "Come to me, all you who weary" (Matt. 11:28 NIV).

Jesus gives the invitation to those whose burdens are too heavy, more than they can carry. "Take my yoke upon you and learn from me" (Matt. 11:29 NIV). When the load gets too heavy and the road too rough, team up with me, He says.

The journey of slavery was too long; the load was too heavy to pull. Slaves discovered that they needed along the dusty roads a companion. When the road was rough and the cross heavy, they needed the cross-bearer. King Jesus was always the answer. King Jesus was always able to supply every need.

When they went to King Jesus, they found grace for weariness and help for the heavy load. They would sing: "Walk on, kind Savior; no man can hinder me." Slaves could say in the midst of heavy loads

> Hold out to the end.
> Hold out to the end.
> It is my determination
> To hold out to the end.

King Jesus gave them power to hold on when they came to the end of their strength.

REFUSING GOD WITHOUT KNOWING IT

> When you refused to help the least of these my brothers,
> you were refusing help to me.
>
> —Matt. 25:45 LBV

Where need is, there is Christ. Christ binds Himself to human need.

The prophet Isaiah: "Surely he hath borne our griefs, and carried our sorrows: yet we did esteem him stricken, smitten of God, and afflicted. But he was wounded for our transgressions, he was bruised for our iniquities; the chastisement of our peace was upon him; and with his stripes we are healed" (Isa. 53:4-5 KJV).

To the Christian, serving God is serving Christ, and serving Christ is serving those in need.

To Christ, religion is outgoing love. Those who win the favor of Christ the King, who will judge nations, are those who become the voice of Christ in preaching glad tidings; the arms of Christ in giving drink to the thirsty, food to the hungry, and clothing to the naked; and the feet of Christ in visiting the sick and the prisoners.

To refuse to meet human need when we have the resources in our possession is to refuse Christ. God is wherever people are oppressed or suffering. He is with:

- The child who has no place to play.
- Those who are cold in slum apartments with rats and roaches.
- The aged person without friends, living on fifty dollars a month in a dingy room.
- Babies dying of hunger.
- The uneducated, unskilled, unwanted, and unemployed.

- The father with five children who was laid off last week and can't pay the rent or feed the kids.
- The bum who is lazy.
- Patients who wait in the clinic all day to be healed.
- Prisoners who sit in jail for six months with no charges brought, waiting for the grand jury.
- The unorganized, without power to change their neighborhoods.
- The brokenhearted.

"When you refused to help the least of these my brothers, you were refusing help to me."

WHEN WE WORSHIP

I was glad when they said unto me, "Let us go to the
house of the Lord."

—Ps. 122:1 RSV

Here am I. Send me.

—Isa. 6:8 NIV

Civilization has not decayed because some people have kept going
to the house of the Lord. Let worship of God cease in His house, and
our world will fall apart.

The Psalm verse is a summary of the impression of a pilgrim who
had been to Jerusalem for worship. He had traveled along with others,
over the rough roads and amid the scorching sun, to join in the feast of
thanksgiving in the temple. Worship had been a soul-stirring experience
for him, so that on the journey back, facing the danger of dark and
lonesome roads, he could say, "I was glad when they said unto me, 'Let
us go to the house of the Lord.'"

Many people find worship an uplifting experience. The queen of
American theater, Helen Hayes, tells of an experience that befell her
in worship. She was facing a terrible ordeal of sorrow. Her beloved
daughter was slowly reaching the final stage of a dreadful disease. The
actress was driven to despair. But while worshiping, she saw trouble
and sorrow in the faces of many other people, and weariness. But they
were drawing on an unfailing source of strength. "They were renewing
their strength," drinking from a spring that refreshed their spirits. In
worship, their faces brightened up. The face of God shone through.

She said that in worship, she gained strength to face her approaching
sorrow. Amid a turbulent storm, she achieved inner peace.

When we worship, God gives us strength to face our dreary days and the turbulent storms of life. With gladness, we go to the house of the Lord so that we can be prepared for the bitter experiences of life.

Jesus went to the synagogue. It was His custom. He went to public worship. He was always in His place in the house of God on the Sabbath.

God's forgiveness is the heart of worship. God cleanses our past. Just as we can pour a bottle of ink into the Mississippi River, and the volume of the water takes up the stain; just as we can open the windows of a car, and the poisonous carbon monoxide gas is cleansed by the flow of pure air, so the love of God in Christ is wide enough and deep enough to sweep out of existence all the guilt and evil that have darkened our lives. We become new creatures because God cleanses us of the old. Worship gives us a sense of forgiveness. God is merciful.

When we worship, we respond to God's call for service. Worship is to prepare us for service. "Then I heard the Lord asking, 'Whom shall I send as a messenger to my people? Who will go?' And I said, 'Lord, I'll go! Send me!'" (Isa. 6:8 TLB).

WORKERS FOR GOD

A pastor had his members put on a slip of paper their answers to this question: who are you working for when you work in the church? There were all kinds of answers. Only one-third of the members responded: "Working for God." That's why Paul deemed it necessary to write to the church of Corinth the message found in the third chapter of his first letter.

You are babies in the Christian life, he said, because you don't understand that you are to follow the Lord. Not Apollos, not Paul. We are not important. Only God is important. We work only for God.

You are only babies being controlled by your own desires, by jealousies, by a hunger for power, for the praise of men, for earthly glory. As a result, you divide up into quarreling and power-seeking groups, defeating the work of Christ in His church.

You are baby Christians until you fully realize that "We are all workers together for God."

The church is not the giant she ought to be today because she has lost sight of who she is and who has established her.

> The Church's one foundation
> Is Jesus Christ her Lord;
> She is His new creation,
> By water and the Word;
> From heaven He came and sought her
> To be His holy bride.
> With His own blood he bought her
> And for her life He died.
> —Samuel J. Stone

The church is a sleeping giant.

Because we have lost sight of the fact that the Christ who established His church is Lord, we fail to give unconditional commitment to Him and His church. We don't recognize Him as a commander.

Some denominations refuse to have one of the great hymns that speaks of the church as the army of Christ in their hymn books. The hymn reminds us that we are soldiers in Christ's army, following Him with His cross as our banner. The church ought to be like a mighty army—the great vision of the hymn writer Sabine Baring Gould says,

> Like a mighty army
> Moves the church of God.
> Brothers, we are treading
> Where the saints have trod.
> We are not divided; all one body we,
> One in hope and doctrine,
> One in charity.

Christ is the commander. Working for the commander, working for God, requires real commitment, unconditional commitment.

In the marriage ceremony, a man commits himself to take the woman as his wife—for better or worse, for richer or poorer, in sickness and in health, unconditionally.

Jesus is not our Lord, our commander, when we work for Him only when it is convenient, when we feel like it, or when the weather is favorable.

The church is weak when we have workers who push the commander aside and follow their own desires and notions, who crave power and the glory of persons.

The church is weak when we have workers who don't have a sense of urgency, zeal, and excitement in the Lord's work, who allow slackness to spoil their work.

The church is weak when we have workers who think they are honoring God by working in the church.

The church is weak when people are more concerned with the honor of serving than the effectiveness of their service.

Our Lord demands unconditional commitment.

In the army, when the commander orders "March!," soldiers march.

Christ is the commander. He is Lord. We are workers for God when we work for Him. Notice that Paul emphasizes working together for God.

The church divided cannot be a mighty army for God. Ministers are asked, "How many members? How many are active?" All of them reply, "Half of them working to build the church and half working to tear it down. Half of them working to lift the church as a light, and the other half putting the light out; half of them trying to give the church a good name in the community, the other half giving the church a black eye; half of them trying to work for God, and the other half working for the devil."

You are not working for God if members are not working in harmony with others to move the church like a mighty army.

Say to the <u>unchurched</u>

> Onward, then, ye people, join our happy throng,
> Blend with ours your voices in the triumphant song,
> Glory, laud and honor unto Christ the King,
> This through countless ages—man and angels sing.
> Onward, Christian soldiers,
> Marching as to war,
> With the cross of Jesus
> Going on before.
>
> —Sabine Baring-Gould

The Cross of Jesus
That CROSS which represents Redeeming Love.
That CROSS which lifts us from the miry clay and plants us on a rock to stay.
That CROSS stained with blood so divine—but which shows us a wondrous beauty.
That CROSS on which Jesus suffered and died to pardon and sanctify me.

That CROSS from which He'll call me one day to my home
far away.
That CROSS I will cherish
Till my trophies I lay down.
That CROSS I will cling to
Until one day I'll exchange it for a crown.

—George Bennard

MAKING ROOM FOR JESUS

It was a strange world where the greatest soul who ever lived was forced to be born in a lowly stable. He was born in a lowly place because there was no room in a high place. He was born among animals because there was no room for Him among men.

In fact, all through His life, wherever He went, He was constantly shut out. No words were more familiar to Him than "no room." Even when He left this world, it was written of Him: "He came unto His own and His own received Him not" (John 1:11 KJV). Most of the people who did know Him had no room for the anointed Savior.

As we read Luke's account of the birth of Jesus, many of us become upset that the world in that day was not prepared for the coming of a Savior foretold by the prophets. But in that day, the people were looking for a different kind of leader. Christ was the kind of leader the world did not expect and was not really prepared for. People were prepared for a leader of force, one who would crush their enemies. But God sent them a Christ to love their enemies and to teach them to love enemies rather than crush them.

The world in that day was not ready for that kind of leader, and the world in our day is not ready for that kind of a leader. That world shut Him out, and our world is likewise shutting Him out.

We have not made room for Him in our race relations. After nineteen hundred years of teaching and preaching that God is the Father of all mankind and all persons are precious in His sight, we are divided by race.

In Christ there is no east or west,
In Him no south or north,
But one great fellowship of love,
Throughout the whole wide earth.
—John Oxenham

That's what we sing, but we are not bound together and we refuse to join hands as one race. Although we proclaim that ours is one nation under God, we maintain two communities—one black and one white. Even more than two today.

Despite the emphasis on the Word inside and outside of church buildings, the essential word embodied in Christ—love—is overshadowed by hate.

We have not made room for the Christ child in our race relations—and not only in race relations. We have not made room for Jesus in our economic order.

As Jesus wept when He looked at Jerusalem—the poor exploited by the rich—He must weep when He looks at our economic order today—poverty in the midst of riches; hunger in the midst of waste; curable diseases in the midst of medical resources. The poor get poorer and the rich get richer. We have crowded the Christ of love and justice out of race relations and our economic order.

Christ and Christmas come, reminding us to make room for the Christ child. Make room in our world. Make room in our lives.

Christ is crowded out of our world because He is crowded out of the lives of people. We become so wrapped up in our little world that we push the eternal world aside. We become so busy doing our own thing that we forget His thing. We are so anxious to please earthly persons that we overlook that Christ is the one we most need to please.

We need to remove the "No Room" sign in our lives for the Christ child. Our lives ought not to be so overcrowded with getting things and the joyous festivities of Christmas that we crowd out Jesus.

We need to make room for Jesus throughout the year, not only at Christmas.

Making room for Jesus means making room for love. Hate shuts Him out.

Making room for Jesus means making room for humility. Pride shuts Him out.

Making room for Jesus means making room for generosity. Greed shuts Him out.

Making room for Jesus means making room for brotherhood and sisterhood. Prejudice shuts Him out.

Making room for Jesus means making room for equality. Inequality shuts Him out.

For He is the Lord of all persons, black, white, and red; the poor and the rich; the learned and the unlearned. He loves us all. He died for us all. He arose for us all. He lives for us all.

Making room for Jesus means making room for others.

WILL CHRISTMAS COME?

For 1,969 years, men have inquired "Will Christmas ever come?" Not the birthday of the King but the promise of the prophets—of peace on earth and justice, the day when the crooked shall be made straight and the rough places plain.

After more than nineteen hundred centuries, the promise of Christmas as a transforming world experience seems only a promise. Men are still wicked. Bitterness has not ceased. Strife grows. With the advancement of technical knowledge, wars increase.

Men glory not in understanding and knowing the God of justice and righteousness, but in their wisdom, their might, their riches.

Christmas appears to be a long way off, not to be in sight—the real Christmas. Many of us have settled down to the celebration of Christmas as a day. We sing the glad tidings without experiencing the gladness. We say the words "peace on earth" without having peace in our own lives. We give gifts to relatives and friends without knowing the great gift of God. We celebrate only the day—not the experience. We hear the sounds and see the sights, but fail to feel the saving power of the Savior.

Will Christmas come to you? Not until Christ comes into your life. You can display beautiful Christmas lights, send warm Christmas greetings, give expensive Christmas gifts, listen to Christmas carols, even read the gospel stories, but it will not come until Christ comes into your life. Christ has come into the world. The world has not received him.

John said, "But as many as received him, to them gave he power to become the sons of God, even to them that believe on his name" (John 1:12 KJV). Those who receive him are given his fullness and grace for grace.

Though rejected through the ages, Christ has come. The light of the world is among us. Things may appear dark and gloomy in our world, but the light of Christ can radiate in our hearts. Christ has come to be in us, to still the storm in our lives. Christ has come to reconcile our contradictions, to harmonize our discords. Christ has come to heal our diseases, to save us from our sins. Christ has come as the torch of truth, the anchor of hope, the pillar of faith, the rock of strength, the refuge for security, the fountain for refreshment, the vine for gladness, the friend for counsel. He has come to be among us and within us.

Will Christmas come to you? Yes, if you let him into your life as ruler.

INWARD POWER TO MATCH OUTWARD TENSION

Come to me, all of you who are tired from carrying your heavy loads, and I will give you rest.

—Matt. 11:28 GNT

The water that I will give him will become in him a spring which will provide him with living water.

—John 4:14 GNT

In these days of ever-increasing tension, we need to find resources that can help us to stand. Millions are faltering under the strain and pressures of life. We are uptight—real tight and can't get unloosed!

The reason so many people break down today is not simply strain, but strain with inadequate power. They don't have inward power to match outward tension. Intake is not equal to output.

Tension occurs when our roots are not deep enough to stand the tempests. Many today are like trees without deep roots when high winds occur.

Millions are severely tensed because of a sense of inadequacy in a time of high winds. Morale is low because they know that tempests can shake the foundation on which they stand.

Much of the tension cannot be eliminated. In work, we will be confronted with it. We will face it in family and other personal relationships. Sickness: a twenty-three-year-old lady is afraid of surgery. Real sorrow: a father has a lovely five-year-old daughter killed by car in front of his own house. He carries her shattered body into the home.

Jesus warned that "in this world, you will have trouble" (John 16:33 NIV). Troubles cause tension. Outward tension cannot be eliminated in this world.

Since tension cannot be eliminated, what we need is power to match it—inward power to match outward tension.

Jesus is constantly saying to us stumbling under the pressures of life, "Come to me, all of you who are weary and burdened, and I will give you rest." He empowers us with adequate strength to face outward tension.

"But the water that I shall give him shall be in him a well of water springing up into everlasting life" (John 4:14 KJV). The woman of Samaria noted that the well she was drawing water from was deep, but she later recognized that the living water Jesus provided was also from a deep well. It was anchored in eternity. The well never runs dry.

This is why the power He provides us is adequate. He is an unfailing well. He offers power for our daily needs, making us deep wells.

What we need to become to face outward tension is a deep well with living water flowing into our lives. When we are anchored deep in living water, we have roots that tempests cannot shake.

Perhaps the problem with many of us is that living water cannot flow into our lives because the pipe is clogged up with fear and doubt. "The Lord is my light and my salvation; whom shall I fear?" (Ps. 27:1 KJV). Doubt clogs the line.

The woman of Samaria first doubted Jesus. Finally, she said, "Give me this water!" (John 4:15 NIV). The woman left her water jar and ran into the city, saying, "Come, see a man!" (John 4:29 NIV). She found in Him the answer to her tension. Christ poured streams of joy into her soul.

When water from the living fountain flowed into her life, she found inward power to match her outward tension. Like the poet, she could say,

> I heard the voice of Jesus say,
> Come unto Me and rest,
> Lay down, thou weary one, lay down
> Thy head upon My breast.
> I came to Jesus as I was,
> Weary, and worn, and sad;
> I found in Him a resting place,
> And He has made me glad.

I heard the voice of Jesus say,
Behold I freely give
The living water; thirsty one,
Stoop down, and drink, and live.
I came to Jesus and I drank
Of that life-giving stream:
My thirst was quenched, my soul revived,
And now I live in Him.
I heard the voice of Jesus say,
I am this dark world's light:
Look unto Me: thy morn shall rise,
And all the day be bright.
I looked to Jesus and I found
In Him my star, my sun;
And in that light of life I'll walk
Till trav'ling days are done."

      —Horatius Bonar

Something within me that holdeth the reins,
Something within me that banishes pain
Something within me I cannot explain.
All that I know there is something within.

      —Lucie E. Campbell

NEVER KNOCKED OUT

But this precious treasure—this light and power that now shine within us—is held in a perishable container, that is, in our weak bodies. Everyone can see that the glorious power within must be from God and is not our own. We are pressed on every side by troubles, but not crushed and broken. We are perplexed because we don't know why things happen as they do, but we don't give up and quit. We are hunted down, but God never abandons us. We get knocked down, but we get up again and keep going.

—2 Cor. 4:7-9 LBV

It was said that slaves on many plantations in North Carolina never knew when they were beaten. They refused to surrender to their foes, who again and again thought that they had conquered them and led them to "stand still."

Those slaves had their eyes on freedom and were confident that God would not let them stand alone as they pursued a noble goal. They were indestructible and invincible.

This is how it was with the apostle Paul. Slight of stature, he was in frail health, afflicted with some malady, but the spirit could not be crushed. Like all of us, he had to struggle with weariness and temptation. He became irritable and resentful at times. He, like us, had his doubts and fears. He had his ups and downs, and his high moments and lows, yet there was something within him that was indestructible. Throw him down, and he bounced up again like a rubber ball. His enemies threw stones and knocked him down, and thought that he was dead or least half dead. But in no time, he was on his feet. They could not destroy him. He had a power within that was endless.

How magnificent is the power God releases in those weak and frail tents of ours! Because of God's power within us, we have the ability to rise above adversities and master them. There is no burden or sorrow or sickness so great that we cannot come out on top of it as more than conquerors with His power. No misfortune can defeat us.

I was visiting the hospital some years back, when a young lady spoke to me and reminded me that she was the one I visited several times at Wesley Long Hospital. She was in an accident and her neck was broken, causing complete paralysis. She was a patient for seven months. For five months, she was not able to move any part of her body. She had setback after setback, but had something within that caused her to keep hope alive. Her courage was endless. She could eventually move two fingers.

It so happened I was there when her father rolled her out of the hospital after nine-and-a-half months. She fought step by step for her recovery and independence.

The apostle Paul, an example of courage, in our text describes the Christian life as mixed with our infirmities, our weaknesses, and with God's glory. He lists a series of paradoxes.

"We are pressed on every side by troubles, but we are not crushed and broken."

Every day we are troubled by something. If something bad does not happen to us, it will happen to some relative, and if not to some relative, then to some dear friend.

We are troubled by what is happening around us: in our community, the increased use of drugs by young people; the robberies (even by teenagers); the killing of innocent people (as in Oklahoma City); children having children; the breakup of families; the lack of concern for the suffering. But Jesus said, "In the world, you have tribulation; but be of good cheer, I have overcome the world" (John 16:33 RSV). Paul is saying: don't let trouble crush you. It may get you down, but don't let it keep you down. There is always power available.

Trouble may hem the body in, but the soul can reach out and commune with the ever-present God of the universe.

In the second paradox, we are not only pressed by troubles on every side, but we are perplexed because we don't know why things happen as they happen. One of the disturbing things about some trouble is that we don't understand it. We don't understand why bad things happen to us. We are puzzled. Why did God permit this or that to happen? We are constantly asking, Why, Lord? Why, Lord? Much we cannot understand and never will in this life. But Paul says we must not give up and quit doing our best. Keep on keeping on though we are puzzled by what happens to us.

The third paradox is that we are persecuted by men (and women). Christians are persecuted—it seems sometimes that people get a kick out of annoying, vexing, and tormenting those who try to do right. They constantly seek ways to drag them down and even to destroy them.

We are persecuted by men and women, but we are never abandoned by God. Persons may let us down, but God always stands by us when we serve Him. It is better to have the blessings of God than the praise of men and women. It is better to be on God's side than to be on man's side. It is better to be alone with God than to be in the company of earthly friends. His love will always abide. The psalmist says, "When my father and my mother forsake me, then the Lord will take me up" (Ps. 27:10 KJV).

If we must stop in a dark sea of clouds, we know that behind the cloud stands God. God never abandons us.

Finally, Paul said, "We are knocked down, but we are never knocked out."

One of the supreme marks of a Christian is that when he or she falls down, he or she does not stay down. Every time he or she falls, he or she rises again.

It is not that he or she is never beaten. Life beats us, but never defeats us.

Sickness knocks us down, but never knocks us out.

The death of our loved ones knocks us down, but never knocks us out.

Failure knocks us down, but never knocks us out.

Being abandoned by friends knocks us down, but never knocks us out.

Persecution knocks us down, but never knocks us out.

Adversity knocks us down, but never knocks us out.

Sin knocks us down, but never knocks us out.

We are never beaten by these—they never knock us out—when the power of the risen Christ is within us.

We are never knocked out when that power is within us. We have resurrection power within us. With that power, we may lose the battle, but we never lose the war.

The power of the risen Christ is sufficient for life. It is sufficient for death. That power lifts us from sinking sand and puts us on a rock. That power lifts us from the grave and takes us into eternity. It is that power which let Paul declare—unafraid, bold, and courageous—when the chopping block was set in position for his execution, the balcony around the courtyard packed with spectators:

"I have fought long and hard for my Lord and through it all I have kept true to Him. And now the time has come for me to stop fighting and rest. In heaven a crown is waiting for me which the Lord, the righteous Judge, will give me on that great day of his return. And not just to me but to all of those whose lives show that they are eagerly looking forward to His coming back again" (2 Tim. 4:7-8 LBV).

FACING LIFE'S DETOURS

And we know that in all things God works for the good
of those who love Him.

—Rom 8:28 NIV

In traveling on our modern highways, we see numerous signs offering warning and directions to travelers. Such is also the case as we travel life's highway.

Perhaps one of the most unpopular signs we confront in traveling is the detour sign. Once you see it, you know that your pace of travel will be slowed down. You also know that the traveling will be rough. There is no use turning back, and you can't go straight ahead. The detour sign is an order to leave the main highway.

Just as there are detours on highways, so there are detours in life. There are times when we must reroute our travel. Life does not always turn out as we plan it. Those dead-end roads in life are as the ones on the highway. They are roads that don't lead anywhere.

Don't stay on a dead-end road—a road where a bridge has been washed out—that is, if you want to go anywhere. A detour road is used to get travelers back on the main road.

Bridges are washed out in life. Accidents occur that defeat our plans. There are times when life must be readjusted—military service, sickness, loss of parent or spouse, shattered dreams.

Remember that detours are temporary rerouting. The main highway is still there, and the detour road leads back to the main highway. Don't settle down on detour roads. Many never get back on the main road. Life's plans are abandoned. Goals are pushed aside. Don't let detours in life cause you to lose sight of your goals. Make adjustments, but press toward the goal of making life count for something.

Remember that God works with us when we face life's detours. When our plans must be readjusted, God works with us. When the bridges wash out and our travel is paralyzed, God works with us. When our dreams and our hopes are shattered, God works with us. We are not prepared to meet life with all of life's detours, the disappointments, the setbacks, the frustrations, the defeats, but with God, we are able.

We are not able to master life with its rough and rocky roads. With God's help, we are able. He helps us to get back on the main highway as we travel life's detour roads. For we know that in all things God works for good with those who love Him.

THE DARK MILE

Even when walking through the dark valley of death
I will not be afraid, for You are close beside me, guarding,
guiding all the way.

—Ps. 23:4 TLB

About three in the afternoon Jesus cried out in a loud
voice . . . "My God, my God, why have you forsaken me?"
—Matt. 27:46 NIV (Fourth Word from the Cross)

All of us sooner or later will have to travel the road of anguish, pain, grief, and loneliness. It is a dark mile. The days are blows and the nights are daggers. It is a path leading to frustration and weakness.

Hope is likely to give in to despair, and faith to fear. It is a time when the valley is lonesome and the agony of our sense of loneliness becomes unbearable.

Even our Lord, as He faced the dark mile of Calvary and death, sensed loneliness in a manner that caused Him to feel forsaken by God the Father. "My God, my God, why have you forsaken me?" He was plunged so far in outer darkness that God seemed for the moment withdrawn.

It was a dark mile not only for our Lord, but for mankind. There was darkness over all the land. The late Peter Marshall describes it: "It was strangely dark. A thunderstorm was blowing up from the mountains and the clouds hid the sun. People looked up at the sky and became frightened. It was an uncanny darkness."

We cannot understand why Jesus felt forsaken by God. He who is God forsaken by God. It is impossible for us to understand this cry of our Lord.

One thing it does is to help us understand how He can in some measure relate to our anguish, pain, grief, and loneliness. We can know that He understands when our way is dark. He understands when the daylight fades into deep night shades.

He knows what it is to feel forsaken. Before the cross, He was forsaken in Nazareth, His hometown. He was forsaken by the nation He came to save. His disciples had forsaken Him. Traveling the darkest of roads, the feeling prevailed for a moment that God had turned from Him. He had withdrawn the sunlight. He had denied His presence.

We can know that when we travel our dark roads of pain, grief, frustration, weakness, and loneliness that our Lord understands.

Another thing we learn from our Lord's experience of traveling the dark road is that though we feel alone, we are never alone; though we feel forsaken, we are never forsaken.

When we walk the dark road of trouble and no light is visible, no love is sensed, our Lord helps us to understand that whatever stands against us, God is for us and will provide resources to help us keep traveling the dark and lonesome road.

Whatever stands against us, God stands above us, around us, and beneath us. We are always surrounded by a love that will not let us go. We can never get away from our God. He precedes us and follows us. "For even darkness cannot hide from God," the psalmist says. "The night shines as bright as day (Ps. 139:12 TLB).

Jesus shows us how to walk the dark mile. In his darkest hour, He held firmly the hand of God. Nothing could break the solid grip.

He had confidence that if the Father stood beside Him, nothing could prevail against Him. He had confidence that the cross itself could not dispose of Him if the Father stood beside Him.

We can have the assurance that nothing can prevail against us if we put our hands in God's hand and keep them there.

It might be necessary for us to tarry in the dark, but we need to keep a solid grip on God's hand.

The long, dark mile that we have to travel can sometimes cause us to want to turn loose God's hand.

The way is rough and rocky. The darkness of the road hides God's face, but His hand is there to guide us and to guard us. His hand becomes a strong staff on which we can lean. His hand leads us as we travel the darkest mile.

The psalmist says, "Even when walking through the dark valley of death I will not be afraid, for You are close beside me, guarding, guiding all the way."

On the other side of the valley is light. Some people stop too soon. A family drove up a mountain road. After driving several miles and seeing nothing exciting, the family turned around and went back. Next day the family was invited to go along with another family to see the beautiful scenery. "It's a sight you'll never forget," the second family said.

The first family was puzzled and confessed that it had already traveled the road and had seen nothing exciting.

"How far did you go?" the second family inquired. "Only to the ridge," the first family said.

"You turned around too soon," the second family replied. "If you had gone a quarter of a mile farther, you would have seen the most beautiful scene to be seen anywhere. You see, you stopped too soon."

Keep traveling!

WHEN LIFE BEGINS TO FALL APART

> We are troubled on every side, yet not distressed; we are
> perplexed, but not in despair; persecuted, but not forsaken;
> cast down, but not destroyed.
>
> —2 Cor. 4:8-9 KJV

> I will lift up mine eyes unto the hills, from whence
> cometh my help. My help cometh from the Lord which
> made heaven and earth.
>
> —Ps. 121:1-2 KJV

One of the first things we need to learn about life is that life is a struggle. There is no escape from the struggles of life. It's a struggle to live. It's a struggle to be decent; it's a struggle to be truthful and honest. It's a struggle to be a decent person. It's a struggle to get along in the home. It's a struggle to get along with our neighbors; it's a struggle to keep some of our promises. It's a struggle to attain a degree of sanity in an insane world.

Our world is moving toward insanity in spite of educational and religious advancement.

We spend billions exploring Mars and the moon, and are not able to stop the drugs coming into our nation—causing mass killing, mental illness, and a sense of insecurity in communities.

As for our sense of values, isn't it a shame that we lift entertainment above educational, scientific, and sociological achievement? The anniversary of a dead entertainer attracts more attention and news coverage than a president, a civil rights leader, or a medical scientist who has found procedures to extend the lives of untold numbers of people.

Life is a struggle, and in our struggles, we sometimes get weary. We find ourselves pressed on every side by troubles. We spend many hours listening to persons weekly who have troubles on top of troubles. Life has not been kind to them. Everything seemed to have gone wrong in spite of their attempts to be decent, be faithful, be helpful. Their lives are falling apart.

There will come times in all of our lives when everything seems to go wrong. After we have done almost our best, we are at our wit's end. We cannot see where life is leading us and cannot understand what can be done to change the course of our lives. All of us have days of darkness of the soul, when darkness seems to hide the inner light. We feel beaten by life and wonder if life is worth living.

Increasing numbers of people commit suicide because the struggle to survive becomes too difficult. Untold number resort to drugs and drinking to attempt to drown out their troubles.

In Paul's words in 2 Corinthians 4, we have a paradox. Someone once said, "Life is like a football game—back and forth, up and down the field." The Negro spiritual "Nobody Knows the Trouble I've Seen" captures the spiritual cry: "I'm sometimes up and sometimes down, O my Lord! I'm sometimes almost on the ground, O my Lord!"

Paul says we are weak as Christians, but we need to know where our strength comes from. We need to know where to turn when life is falling apart.

Christ is able to empower us so that we often suffer but we are never crushed. Even when we don't know what to do, we never give up. In times of trouble, God is with us. We never have to stand alone. When we are knocked down, we get up again. We are cast down, our hearts are made to bleed, but we are never destroyed. We learn from Jesus how to face life when it falls apart. When life is grim, look to the hill.

Jesus Himself in Gethsemane, at a grim time in His life, facing death, cries to the Father, "May this cup be taken from me!" (Matt. 26:39 NIV). We pray, in our grim moments in life, "Let this cup pass from me!"

Jesus Himself had to learn how to accept what He could not fully understand, and was still able to say, "God, Thou art love." I build my faith on that.

Paul faced everything—suffering, death—with courage because he believed that even death could not destroy him. He had drawn upon that power that was sufficient for life and greater than death.

God's power is sufficient to help us conquer suffering and gain victory over the grave.

Jesus promised His disciples—those who followed Him, drew upon His power, and served Him—that He would never abandon them. He promised never to leave them.

> I've seen the lightning flashing,
> I've heard the thunder roll.
> I've felt sin's breakers dashing,
> Trying to conquer my soul;
> I've heard the voice of my Savior,
> Telling me still to fight on.
> He promised never to leave me,
> Never to leave me alone.
>
> —Ludie D. Pickett

I trust in that promise, and I will trust in that promise until I die. Death will not conquer.

WHEN WE REACH THE
BREAKING POINT

Most people reach points in life when life seems unbearable. They face:

1. Family conflicts and disappointments.
2. Pressures of the job.
3. Financial crises.
4. Physical suffering; they have suffered enough and are worn and weary.
5. Struggles with enemies.

Someone once said, "I wish I had a plastic heart so that I could escape the anguish of it being broken." But the truth is we don't. We have hearts that can be crushed and broken. We are creatures with spirits that can be beaten, twisted, and frustrated. Our dreams can be shattered. Our plans can fail. Our hopes can dissolve. Things we learn to lean upon can crumble away.

We can reach the breaking point in life's experiences. Life can seem unbearable at times. What then?

The Bible has a word for us when we reach the breaking point, when our best is not good enough, when seemingly we have come to the end of the road, when we find ourselves unable to stand up to life.

God has a Word:

Moses: "The eternal God is your Refuge, and underneath are the everlasting arms" (Deut. 33:27 TLB).

God has a Word:

The psalmist: "Wait for the Lord, be strong, and let your heart take courage; yea, wait for the Lord" (Ps. 27:14 RSV).

God has a Word:

The psalmist again: "though the mountains shake in the heart of the sea; though its waters roar and foam; though the mountains tremble" (Ps. 46:2-3 RSV) "The Lord of hosts is with us; the God of Jacob is our refuge" (Ps. 46:11 KJV). "He will give his angels charge of you to guard you in all your ways. On their hands they will bear you up, lest you dash your foot against a stone" (Ps. 91:11-12 RSV).

God has a Word:

The prophet Isaiah: "He gives power to the faint, and to him who has no might he increases strength" (Isa. 40:29 RSV).

God has a Word:

The apostle Paul: "I can do all things through Christ which strengtheneth me" (Phil. 4:13 KJV).

Again: "Let us run with perseverance the race marked out for us. Let us fix our eyes on Jesus, the author and perfecter of our faith" (Heb. 12:1-2 NIV).

The psalmist in the twenty-seventh division affirms his faith and hope that God will, in this life, grant him the favor he prays for. Although the sky is dark, and in distress he cries for deliverance, yet he finds courage in his trouble to wait on the Lord.

This is the first thing we must learn to do when we come to the breaking point: wait on the Lord, hold on a little longer. We are prone to place a time limit on God's response to our cries for help. God moves in His time, not ours. He will deliver us. He will help us to be patient. He gives power to the faint.

Second, not only must we wait, but we must turn the corner. We don't know what God has waiting for us around the corner.

BACK TO GOD

Draw near to God, and He will draw near to you.
—James 4:8 RSV

James, the brother of Jesus, summons those who are professed Christians to return to God. They, like millions in our day, had strayed from God even while remaining in the Christian fellowship. They belonged to the church, but were not in the church. To be in the church is to have the church in us. To have the church in us is to have the indwelling Spirit of God within us.

Calling on Christians to return to God presupposes spiritual back-sliding. Like the sheep who nibbled on grass and moved to other patches until he found himself lost, so Christians had inched and inched in the life of the world until they were away from God.

The summons of James is one that is still relevant. The professed Christians of our day have lost their bearing. We have lost our sense of direction. We have lost respect for truth, justice, and goodness.

We place men on the moon, but fail to place millions in decent houses. We build a lodging place for men in space, but fail to deal meaningfully with the problems of men on earth. We find fuel to man aircraft to bomb innocent mothers and babies, but fail to find fuel to keep mothers and babies warm in our country.

We, like the president of our nation, announce one day that we will have our way, and then hold prayer breakfasts to ask God to make our will His will for us.

We get involved in scandals, and then ask that investigations designed to reveal the facts be curbed.

We sing and pray on Sunday, but offer God counterfeit love and faith on Monday. We claim to love Him, but commit spiritual adultery by adulterating our love for Him. We don't love Him as God, but as youngsters love Santa Claus. We resist His demands upon us, and rebel against His laws.

We want Him as Savior, but not as our Lord. You see, when He is Lord of our lives, He comes first.

We have drifted from God. We have lost our bearings. Thank God, however, that there is a path back to God!

"Draw near to God, and He will draw near to you." We must have power to commit our total lives to our Lord.

> All to Jesus I surrender.
> Lord, I give myself to Thee;
> Fill me with Thy love and power.
> Let Thy blessing fall on me.
> I surrender all, I surrender all;
> All to Thee, my blessed Savior, I surrender all.
>
> —Judson W. Van De Venter

FORGIVENESS IS COSTLY

To fully realize what God has done for us in Christ, we must realize that forgiveness comes at a tremendous price.

So often, forgiveness has been presented as an easy gospel. In this day, when there is so much sin and so great a need for forgiveness, we try to make believe that it comes easy. It is hard to forgive sins—hard for us, hard for Christ.

"Which is easier," asked Jesus in the story of the man with palsy, "to say, 'Your sins are forgiven,' or to say, 'Get up and walk'?" (Luke 5:23 NIV). It is easier to tell a man with palsy to walk. It is easier to meet any other human need than to say, "Thy sins are forgiven."

Perhaps that sounds strange from Jesus. We have generally thought that it was easy for Him to forgive. He said so many wonderful words about forgiveness; He demonstrated it so strikingly on the cross: "Father forgive." But it was hard for Him to forgive, as it always ought to be. We Christians need to learn that forgiveness is required of us but that it is hard to do and very costly.

Why is it hard? Why was it hard for Jesus to forgive? In the first place, because He took sin seriously. It is easy to condone sin, to make light of it; but when one takes it seriously, it is hard to forgive.

Suppose a person specialized in growing flowers and prized them more than anything else. Suppose someone went into his flower garden and ignorantly trampled them all down, spoiling something that represented labor, money, and joy. Of course someone who didn't value flowers would make light of it. But for one who loved and valued flowers, forgiveness would not be easy. It would be painful.

Today, we often take lightly the sexual sins displayed in movies and on TV programs. But we grit our teeth when a fine girl is destroyed in virtue. It is hard to forgive if we cherish the virtue in the girl. It is painful.

When you hear anyone talking of forgiveness as an easy matter, you can be sure he is not forgiving sin; he is condoning it. To say that sin does not matter is to condone sin. Our generation is increasingly guilty of condoning moral looseness by saying that sin does not matter. Sin does matter. Yes, it is easy to condone sin, but painful and costly to forgive.

An example of the difference is shown in two kinds of mothers today. One mother demonstrates a false love for her son by a lack of seriousness about his moral life. When her son wallows in vice, she will receive him again, making light of the sin, saying that it does not matter. She will make up more excuses for him than he can himself.

The other mother never could forgive a son who wallows in vice in that way. She will be sympathetic and forgive him, but will take his vice seriously. It would pain her heart and she would bear upon her the outrage of his sin as though she had committed it herself. She would stand at the door grief-stricken, awaiting his return. She would forgive him, but it would turn her hair gray. She would put herself in his place and would bear the burden of the guilt. This is forgiveness. It always means pain and self-substitution. "Christ was innocent of sin, and yet for our sake God made him one with the sinfulness of men" (2 Cor. 5:21 NEB).

In the second place, Jesus found it hard to forgive because He loved people. Ah, you say, the love of people makes it easy to forgive.

When you love someone deeply and another's sin hurts that person, it is hard to forgive. And sin always does hurt to other people. Nobody sins unto himself alone. Alcoholics hurt parents, wives, children—somebody else is hurt. When one cares for people as Jesus did, it is hard to forgive sin.

Joseph's brothers dropped him into a pit, hauled him out again, and sold him as a slave to a band of Midianites bound for Egypt, dipping his long-sleeved cloak in the blood of a goat and carrying the cloak back to Jacob, the father, trying to persuade him that Joseph was dead. Suppose they had felt compelled to go to Jacob, confessing their sin in mistreating Joseph, and had sought forgiveness. The first question that the father would ask in grief: where is Joseph? You ask me to forgive you, but your sin is not simply between me and you. Where is Joseph? How can I forgive you until I know that all is well with Joseph?

When you love people, it is hard to forgive sin.

In the gospels, you find it is hard for Jesus. He was severe on the scribes and Pharisees—woe unto you. Beware of the scribes and Pharisees who destroy widows' houses. Jesus was thinking of the widows.

It is hard to forgive members who destroy the name and consequently the influence of other members. When you care for people, it is hard to forgive sin. It is painful and costly.

Third, forgiveness was supremely costly to Jesus. It was not cheap and easy. Christ put Himself entirely in our place. Human compassion is unable to do this. Only divine compassion is able, and God became man. He emptied Himself of everything but love. The Creator becomes a creature, taking the form of a servant. He humbled himself and went to the cross. He suffered, bled, and died that you and I might be forgiven, reconciled, and made one with Him.

He substituted for us. He put himself in our place so that at the day of judgment—when justice seeks the place where we as sinners stand with all our guilt—it will not find us. We will no longer stand in that place; another will stand in our place—assurance as we look at the cross.

> Blessed assurance, Jesus is mine!
> O what a foretaste of glory divine.
> Heir of salvation, purchase of God.
> Born of His Spirit, washed in His blood.
> This is my story, this is my song,
> Praising my Savior, all the day long;
> His is my story, this is my song,
> Praising my Savior all the day long.
>
> —Fanny Crosby

PUTTING GOD IN THE DRIVER'S SEAT

And ye shall seek me, and find me, when ye shall search
for me with all your heart.

—Jer. 29:13 KJV

You will find me when you seek me, if you look for me
in earnest.

—Jer. 29:13 TLB

Are you playing games with God?

Many church people are playing games with God. They claim to be
seeking God, when actually they are just playing games with God.

They want God to help them over some temporary discomfort.
They look for God to help them when they stand in the roadway
looking for a passing motorist to push them to the next gas station.

They are just playing games with God.

They want God simply to save them from trouble, to heal their
sickness, to give them success in their endeavors, to provide a heaven
after they have stopped playing games with Him.

They want to use God as a means to an end; they want a Santa
Claus.

They love God not because He is God, but because of ways they
hope to exploit His love for them.

They are playing games with God, for they pretend to want God
and at the same time push Him aside. They want Him, but not to
interfere with their business; they want Him, but not to deal with their
secret sins.

There are a lot of us who want Him, but we don't want Him in
the driver's seat. We spend our years fumbling around in the dark with

light surrounding us. Our lives are torn asunder while the peacemaker stands at the gate. We falter under the pressures of life, when the enabler is within us. We burst our brains trying to solve problems when the problem solver is knocking on our door. We are playing games with God.

We are playing with God until we seek Him as God. When we seek Him as God, we let Him in the driver's seat.

Our lives are messed up because we want to stay in the driver's seat. The first thing staying in the driver's seat does is that it keeps us selfish. The most difficult of all sins to overcome is selfishness—I, me, my, I want, my desire, my way, what will happen to me? We need, as the song goes, to say

> Have thine own way, Lord!
> Have thine own way.
> Thou art the potter, I am the clay;
> Mold me and make me after Thy will,
> While I am waiting, yielded and still.
> Have Thine own way, Lord
> Have Thine own way!
> Hold o'er my being absolute sway.
> Fill with Thy Spirit
> Till all shall see
> Christ only, always,
> Living in me.
>
> —Adelaide A. Pollard

We must not be a small packet wrapped up in self. We will have a messed up life until we get rid of selfishness and surrender our lives to God.

The second thing staying in the driver's seat does is that it keeps us in the dark—fearful, anxious, tense, uptight, worrying about what's ahead.

When we surrender and let God in the driver's seat, we can relax and feel secure. He is a driver who knows the dangers ahead and knows how to drive over mountains and through valleys. He knows how to fly through storms.

I don't worry about what's ahead when He's in the driver seat. When we surrender the driver's seat to the pilot of life, we don't sweat about our problems. When we let God become our God, we can turn our problems over to Him. When our lives are surrendered to Him, our problems become His problems.

He doesn't always cast them away, but He gives us wisdom and strength to deal with them. He provides direction and power that we need to cope with problems. That's why we are taught to "Cast all your anxiety on him because he cares for you" (1 Peter 5:7 NIV).

He knows how to deal with our problems. He is able to give grace when the burden is not removable. He is able to bring calmness on the inside when storms rage on the outside.

He is able to keep us from falling and to present us faultless before His presence in glory. He even erases the past so that we no longer feel guilty about our previous evil.

One day, He's going to take me in spite of my past, my weakness, my inadequacies, and present me to God as if I were dressed in His own righteousness.

He died that messed-up people could be safe on the day of judgment. He not only died, but He arose that we would know that He is able to give us the victory—victory over sin, victory over suffering, victory over death.

ONLY ONE LIFE

I have come that they might have life, and have it to the full.

—John 10:10 NIV

There is a popular expression: "I have only one life to live and it is so short."

Life is seemingly short for many of us. We spend our years as a tale that is told. Life is soon cut off, and we fly away.

Even if we are blessed with three score years and ten, life still seems short. In fact, we can subtract about a third of our life span. A third of the time is spent sleeping. Then we can subtract the first one or two years of childhood. In terms of waking hours, we live about twenty-two years if we die at seventy. If we counted the misspent hours of life, life would be dreadfully short. Some people at age seventy will have lived seven or eight years. Some will not really have lived at all.

The thing that makes not living tragic is that there is only one life. We have just one crack at living. The misspent life is lost. A useless life is death.

Life, of course, is not something we choose. The choice to be born is not ours. Neither is death determined by us. The only choice we have is how we live our lives.

How long we live is in the hands of God. How well we live rests with us in great measure. God has made us free agents to choose the way that leads to life or the road that leads away from life.

God provides life, but we must choose it. God stops to mend our brokenness in Christ, to purify our corruption, to release us from captivity, to redeem us in our lostness, but we must accept His offer.

Jesus comes from God to us as a means of giving us life. "I have come that they might have life, and have it to the full." Jesus opens the way to life as He opens the way to God.

God is not only the creator of physical life; He releases life in its fullness. Without Him, we never come to know the beauty, the joy, the fullness of living. Jesus brings the abundant life by leading us ever closer to God.

God offers us only one life, but He draws close to us in Christ to help us make the best of that one life. He first helps us to be true to our gifts. Life is a gift—time, talents, influence, and money. We should use our gifts wisely, not selfishly, and reach our full potential. Life is giving. He who loses his life finds it. Jesus said, "The Father loves me because I lay down my life that I may have it back again" (John 10:17 LBV).

Second, after we shall have lived well in this life, He provides the opportunity for complete fulfillment beyond. Regardless how long we live here on this earth, there is a yearning for something yet not attained.

The complete life is not fully achieved in this world. "What we see now is like the dim image in a mirror; then we shall see face to face. What I know now is only partial; then it will be complete" (1 Cor. 13:12 TEV).

The epistle to the Hebrews pictured the heroes of faith. Paul cited the mighty figures who marched across the stage of Israel's history—Abraham, Moses, David, and the others. Then the author closed with the words "and all these, though well attested by their faith, did not receive what was promised, since God had foreseen something better for us, that apart from us they should not be made perfect" (Heb. 11:39-40 RSV).

We live in three tenses—the past, the present, and the future.

Others have run the course before us. They did not reach the fulfillment of their dreams. We will not attain all of our aspirations, but when we live well, we pave the way for those who follow us to carry out our unfulfilled dreams. Make life count!

OUR BEST AND WORST MEMBER

The story is told of a man who invited some friends to eat with him and sent his servant to the market to buy the best things he could find. When dinner was served, every course consisted of tongue richly prepared with different kinds of sauce. After dinner, the master angrily said to the servant, "What do you mean by serving tongue for every course? Did I not tell you to buy the best food that could be found in the market?" The servant replied, "I have obeyed your orders! There is nothing better than a good tongue. It is the organ with which we speak kindness, pray to God, and spread love and friendship among persons."

The next day the master sent the servant to market for some food to feed the dogs. "Get me the worst things you can find," he ordered. When the servant returned with tongues again, the master cried out, "What! You dare not bring tongue again!" "Most certainly," answered the servant. "There is nothing worse than a bad tongue. It is the organ that speaks lies and spreads gossip. It says mean things that make people angry with each other. There is nothing as good as a kind tongue. There is nothing as cruel as a bad tongue."

The tongue can be our worst member, or the tongue can be our best member. It can be used to curse our fellow travelers, or it can be used to bless and praise God. James in his letter speaks of the tongue as "a flame of fire" that "can turn our whole lives into a blazing flame of destruction and disaster" (James 3:6 LBV). The unknown author of the poem "The Tongue" says, "The Greeks declare: the boneless tongue, small and weak, can crush and fill. The Persians: a lengthy tongue and early death. The Arabs declare: the tongue can speak a word whose speed outstrips the steed."

"Death and life are in the power of the tongue" (Prov. 18:21 RSV). It is impossible to determine the injury wrought by that uncontrolled member of our bodies. Many sins are committed with the tongues—lying, conscious lying, false witness, and gossip.

You can set a whole forest afire by a tiny spark. The tongue is physically small, but can poison a host of bodies. Church people join in spreading evil merchandise from house to house and community to community. Many homes have been broken up through gossip, numerous lives wrecked. Good people have had their reputations destroyed through gossip. The influence of lives has been severely damaged through gossip. Much of the gossip is unfounded. Once scattered, it cannot be stopped.

SOMETHING TO CROW ABOUT

> This is what the Lord says: "Let not the wise man boast of his wisdom or the strong man boast of his strength or the rich man boast of his riches, but let he who boasts boast about this; that he understands and knows me, that I am the Lord, who exercises kindness, justice and righteousness on earth."
>
> —Jer. 9:23-24 NIV

All of us need something to crow about. We need to find something that gives us a sense of importance, a sense of worth. Without it, life becomes meaningless and empty.

This is a season of the year when many parents' hearts are warmed by the educational achievements of their sons and daughters. Their grins are seen from ear to ear as they watch their children parade across the stage to receive diplomas and degrees. It is the culmination of years of sacrifice and struggle of parents. How wonderful it is to hear a mother and father boast after the child has received some award, "That's my child." We like to crow about our grandchildren. We carry "brag books" containing their likenesses.

We want them to do well, and it pleases us deeply when they succeed.

Remember how the mother of James and John asked Jesus to seat her two sons beside Him when He came into His kingdom? The motive was, of course, to afford her the opportunity to brag about her two sons, to say to other mothers, "See, see where my sons are seated."

Churches seek to excel in some program, or to build structures, or even (sometimes) to adopt higher standards for membership in order to have something to crow about.

Nations strive to develop industrial programs or make scientific advancements as a basis for boasting.

Rome could crow about its system of government, Greece about its culture, Germany—at one time—about her military power, Japan (today) about industrial development, America about her creed proclaiming liberty and justice for all (empty in practice).

We are all trying to find something to crow about.

Jeremiah warns us in our text that this is what the Lord says: let not the wise person boast of his or her wisdom, or the mighty person of his or her might, or the rich person of his or her riches. None of these is worthy to crow about or to glory in.

The wise person is limited in his or her wisdom. Only God is all wise. Persons who glory in their wisdom usually make fools of themselves. We always meet someone down the road wiser than we.

Richard Nixon disgraced himself, his family, and nation trying to be wise.

Job found out how foolish he was questioning the wisdom of the almighty God. "Listen to this, Job; stop and consider God's wonders" (Job 37:14 NIV).

Do you know how God controls the clouds and makes His lightning flash? Who is this that darkens my counsel? Where were you, Job, when I laid the earth's foundations? Who marked off its dimensions? Who stretched a measuring line across it? On what were its footings set, or who laid its cornerstone while the morning stars sang together and all the angels shouted for joy?

No person has been, is, or will be wise enough to crow about wisdom. We glory that we know One who is all wise.

Likewise, we ought not to crow about our might. We are weaklings—even those who think they are strong. Most of us cannot control ourselves.

Napoleon, a powerful ruler, conquered Europe, but was never able to conquer himself.

Mighty Samson ought not to be crowed about. We are so limited in our strength.

We ought to crow about wisdom, not power.

We ought not to boast of riches ("let not the rich person boast in his riches") In the first place, riches are only entrusted to us as trustees and stewards.

"The earth is the Lord's and the fulness thereof" (Ps. 24:1 KJV). The rich young ruler became a fool dealing with riches.

Never crow about wealth or material prosperity.

Riches, earthly power, and wisdom are not things we ought to crow about. All of these are only temporary. They are not abiding.

Since we need something to boast of, to crow about, to glory in, where can we turn? "Let him or her boast about this—that he or she truly knows me."

How wonderful it is to truly know Him! The apostle Paul said, "I consider everything a loss compared to the surpassing greatness of knowing Christ Jesus, my Lord" (Phil. 3:8 NIV).

We boast (we crow) that God exercises kindness in dealing with us. That He reaches for us in our lostness. That He picks us up when we fall. That He helps us to face the rough and rocky roads of life. That He makes a way when no way seems possible. That He makes a way somehow.

We boast that though we are weak, He makes us strong; that though we are unworthy, He shows loving kindness; that though we are sinful, we are His children. That we are poor, He is rich. We can crow about facts.

> My Father is rich in houses and lands.
> He holdeth the wealth of the world in His hands!
> Of rubies and diamonds, of silver and gold,
> His coffers are full; He has riches untold.
> —Harriett E. Buell

I can crow about the fact that I've been adopted, my name's written down, an heir to a mansion, a robe and a crown. I'm a child of the King.

TAKING GOD LIGHTLY

Thou shalt not take the name of the Lord thy God in vain.
—Ex. 20:7 RSV (Third Commandment)

It is important that we recognize that the third commandment is more than just a prohibition against swearing. Swearing is one of the ways that the commandment is broken. It is broken by millions every day. Swearing is a vile habit even among Christians. How many times have we heard even in the church persons say, "I swear I am telling the truth"? In recent years, there has been a tolerance for swearing in our nation. In early years, it was frowned on.

Profanity has become almost an acceptable practice. Those who write plays put profanity into their works with the excuse that it reflects life in our world today. We have a lot of dirt in our world, but we still expect people to wash before they sit down and eat.

Swearing and profanity for many people have become thoughtless habits. However, when we swear, we break the third commandment, which says, "Thou shalt not take the name of the Lord thy God in vain." Whenever we use profane language, we take the name of the Lord in vain. When we curse, we profane God with the breath He gives us.

To swear is to try to use God in an unworthy way. To swear is to make a mockery of prayer. Perhaps we have not thought of swearing as a form of prayer, but to swear is to call upon God in an evil way.

The third commandment is also more than a prohibition of perjury—the willful telling of a lie while under oath to tell the truth. From early years, people have tried to insure the truthfulness of a witness by requiring him or her to swear by the name of God that he or she was telling the truth. The logic in the practice is that, if a person called on the name of God, he or she would be afraid to tell a lie lest God's vengeance be visited upon him or her.

The problem is that many persons have no fear of God. God and His laws are taken lightly.

Jesus emphasized a person's work should depend not on his or her swearing, only by his or her integrity. "But I say to you, Do not swear at all either by heaven . . . or by earth" (Matt. 5:34 RSV). "And do not swear by your head, for you cannot make one hair white or black. Let what you say be simply Yes or No; anything more than this comes from evil" (Matt. 5:36-37 RSV).

The third way and perhaps the most far-reaching way we break the third commandment is to take God lightly. To take the name of God in vain is more than swearing or committing perjury or profanity; it is taking God lightly. The name of God is holy because God is holy. "Holy, holy, Lord God almighty."

It is an empty practice to honor God's name unless one's life also honors God. It is not what we say or do not say about God that matters most, but whether we serve Him and live for Him and whether we do His will. It is vain to glorify Him with our words and not glorify Him with our lives. It is vain to say "Lord, Lord," and fail to do His will. It is vain to address Him as our shepherd and stray from the paths on which He leads us. It is vain to sing glory to His name and lift other names above His. It is vain to call Him king and fail to work for His kingdom on earth.

Jesus taught His disciples to pray not only "Our Father, hallowed be Thy name" but also "Thy Kingdom come on earth as it is in heaven."

We live in defiance of God when we fail to seek and do His will. We take Him lightly.

THE ETERNAL WORD

The word of our God will stand forever.

—Isa. 40:8 RSV

The Bible is the most remarkable book in the world. No book can start comparing with it in terms of its popularity or influence. It is in a class altogether by itself.

The Bible is a book for all mankind. It belongs to no cult, no class, no nation, no race. It is not a Jewish book, nor a Roman Catholic book, nor a Protestant book. It is a book for the world.

It was written over a period of fifteen hundred years by inspired men of God. They included all kinds of men: Moses, the lawgiver; Joshua, the militarist; Samuel, the judge and the maker of kings; Job, the poet; David, the shepherd; Haggai, the building contractor; Matthew, the tax collector; Luke, the physician; Peter, the fisherman; Paul, the tent-maker, and John, the dreamer. Yet, with the diversity, there is a marvelous unity of thought and purpose through the Bible.

The Bible deals with vital subjects: how to live, how to suffer, how to succeed, how to conquer evil, how to die, and how to live forever.

It is the book that reveals the mind of God and describes men and women perfectly. It points to the ways of salvation and charts the course of the redeemed.

The Bible is so outstanding that it is called *the Book*.

In a message presented by J. B. Chapman, D.D., on June 16, 1940, at the Tenth General Assembly of the Church of the Nazarene, the following story was told:

An untutored woman sat reading her Bible when a learned skeptic came along and asked, "What is that you are reading?" The woman answered, "It is the Word of God."

"Who told you it is the Word of God?" the skeptic asked. "God told me," she said. "And how did God tell you that?" he asked. The woman was quiet for a moment and then, looking up toward the brilliant sun, she inquired, "What is that?" "It is the sun," the skeptic replied. "Who told you it is the sun?" she asked. "No one need tell me that. It tells me itself. I know it is the sun for it gives me life and light and heat and happiness," the skeptic said. "And that is how God told me this is His Word," the woman said. "It also gives me life and light and heat and happiness. It is its own witness."

The prophet Isaiah, one thousand years before the birth of Christ, understood that the Word was more than words recorded in a book, that the Word of God was embodied in a person—later, what the gospel writer John wrote was made flesh. He proclaimed in the eighth verse of the fortieth chapter KJV that "the word of our God shall stand for ever."

The Bible is not only the Word of God; it is the eternal Word of God. It is the eternal Word of God because the Word is embodied in one who is eternal, one who changes not. "Jesus Christ is the same, yesterday and today and forever" (Heb. 13:8 RSV).

The supreme revelation of the Bible is Jesus Christ. From the first book to the last, there is one goal, one end, that of revealing God through Jesus Christ, who became flesh at Christmas and dwelt among us. Martin Luther speaks of a little Bible. If all of the Bible were eliminated but John 3:16 KJV, it would still have the message of salvation: "For God so loved the world that he gave his only begotten Son, that whosoever believeth in him should not perish, but have everlasting life."

There is for all of us the problem of understanding the Bible. There are so many difficult passages. But what is essential to salvation and to life is clear and plain.

Many are helped by Bible study to understand difficult passages, but the best qualification for understanding the Bible is a willingness to obey it, especially to obey the great commandment given by Jesus Himself: love God and love fellow persons.

Someone once said, "The parts of the Bible that I cannot understand do not trouble me as much as the parts that I can understand."

"In everything do to others what you would have them do to you" (Matt. 7:12 NIV).

The important thing is to realize that the Bible is primarily a book about Christ. The theme itself is the enduring love of God climaxed in the person of Jesus Christ. The Bible comes powerfully alive only when we start with Christ and accept Him as the real hero in the Bible. Every book of the Old as well as the New Testament is centered on Christ.

For instance, in Genesis, Jesus is the "seed of the woman" that bruised the serpent's head. In Numbers, He is the guiding pillar of clouds and fire on the way to the Promised Land. He is the model husband in the book of Ruth. He is the personification of wisdom in Proverbs.

In Isaiah, He is the child born, the son given, the wonderful counselor, the suffering Savior, the Comforter, the Prince of Peace. In Hosea, He is the Redeemer of the unworthy. He is the opener of the cleansing fountain in Zechariah and the purifier of the sons of Levi in Malachi.

In the Bible, Jesus is the answer to every need. To the hungry, He is bread; to the thirsty, He is water; to the sick, He is a physician and healing balm; to the condemned, He brings pardon, and He opens the prison doors to those incarcerated. To those whose lives are wasted, He gives beauty for ashes. He is the rose of Sharon for beauty, the lily of the valley for purity, the morning star of hope, the Lamb of God for atonement, a great rock in a weary land, and a shelter in the time of storm. He is money for the poor, wisdom for the ignorant, and holiness for the defiled. He is the eternal Word! Death could not defeat Him! The grave could not destroy Him! A living Bible and a living Lord.

Hymnist John Newton writes,

> His name yields the richest perfume,
> And sweeter than music His voice.
> His presence disperses my gloom
> And makes all within me rejoice.
> I should, were He always thus nigh,
> Have nothing to wish or to fear.
> No mortal so happy as I,
> My summer would last all the year.

WHAT IS YOUR EXCUSE?

In Luke 14:16-24, Jesus tells the story of a man who prepared a great feast and invited many people. When the dinner was ready, he sent a servant out to remind those who had been invited and to bid them to come. "Please come," he begs each one. "Everything is now ready." But they all began to make excuses.

The first one said to the servant, "I have purchased some land, and must go and look at it. Please excuse me!"

The second man said, "I have just purchased five yoke of oxen, and am on my way to try them out. Please convey my apologies."

Another one said, "I have just got married, and I am sure you can understand my predicament."

Jesus is saying that God invites all of us to enter His kingdom, but like the men invited to the dinner, many of us offer flimsy excuses. Our excuses are basically as flimsy as those given in the parable.

The first excuse was: "I have purchased some land, and must look at it." This excuse is extremely suspect. Who would purchase land without seeing it? We don't make that kind of investment without a whole lot of looking. Without doubt, the man had examined the land many times before he made the purchase.

Look at another excuse given by one of the men: "I have purchased five yoke of oxen and must try them out." In our day, a person who buys a car without trying it out needs to have his head examined. You don't assume the burden of twenty-four or thirty-six monthly payments, plus the old car or down payment on a new one, without testing it out. The excuse of the second man is indeed very thin.

Perhaps the third man had the best excuse of all. He had just married. It is possible that he had accepted the invitation before marriage and did not feel comfortable in a crowd with his new wife.

In a day when men find so little time to spend with even their new wives and families, we find it difficult to quarrel with the third man.

However, the chances are that marriage caused him to lose sight of his obligations and his need of others. Some newly married couples become snobs.

The parable offers us two needed lessons to remember. First, our excuses are flimsy. We hear the call to serve the Christian cause and give to support the kingdom, but we say we don't have time and don't have money. What we really mean is that we don't have time for God. We don't have money for God and His church.

The truth is that when we refuse the invitation to work in His vineyard, we choose the minors over the majors, the secondary over the primary, the less significant over the most important, the second best over the best, self over the kingdom.

Our choices reveal what is really important to us. We can't place too much emphasis today on the importance of choices as we deal with young people.

A bad choice is made, and it becomes too late to correct it. Great opportunities are lost. Potentially great lives are defeated.

Second, God is hurt when we refuse His offer of the best. Parents have some idea how God is hurt by our refusals to accept His offer for the best in life. Parents dream and work for the best opportunities for a child, only to see him choose the worse. Parents crave companionship and get indifference, long for affection from a child and get ingratitude. That hurts. A brokenhearted father said he wore himself down working to provide the best educational opportunities for his boy, who got involved in drugs and became a dropout his first year in college.

That, too, is the hurt in the heart of God. "I taught Ephraim also to go, taking them by their arms, but they knew not that I healed them" (Hos. 11:3 KJV). That hurts. Jesus wept as he looked over Jerusalem. "Ah, if you only knew . . . on what your peace depends—but you cannot see it" (Luke 19:40 PME).

The main message of all religion is that nothing works without God. Nothing can get right in human affairs without God. Without Him, we lose our way. What is your excuse today for refusing Him?

WHEN WE COME TO OUR SENSES

> But when he came to himself he said, "How many of my father's hired servants have bread enough and to spare, but I perish here with hunger!" I will arise and go to my father, and I will say to him, "Father, I have sinned against heaven and before you."
>
> —Luke 15:17-18 RSV

When we think we can make it on our own, we are out of our minds.

When we forget the source of our strength, we are foolishly blind. When we lose sight of whom we are and whose we are, we make a mess out of life.

The major mistake the young boy made was to think that he could withdraw from the father and the father's house and make it. He thought he could make it on his own.

One of the troubling trends today is the trend toward moving away from God. The drift is not always intentional. In the story of the lost sheep, it is apparent that the lost sheep did not intentionally get lost. He nibbled the grass and moved to greener grass without realizing how far he was drifting from the shepherd and other sheep.

The young son did not want to be cut off from the father's security. He just wanted freedom from his control. He didn't want to be fenced in.

The trend of mankind today is not to get away from God as provider, but from God as controller. We don't want God controlling what we do. We want to be free to do what we please.

As with the young son, with that attitude, we drift and drift away until we are in a vital sense cut off from God. God must be all God or no God. He must be all Lord or no Lord at all.

We are out of our minds when we think we can have Him when we want Him and push Him aside when we don't want Him.

The young boy didn't want to get rid of his father as one he could fall back on; he just didn't want him to exercise control as a father.

Does that sound familiar in our day?

Straying away from the father, the boy found himself drifting downward and downward until he was cut off completely.

That is what sin will do for us; it causes us gradually to drift and drift away from God until His power is not felt, His voice is not heard, His light is not seen, His will is not sought.

How wretched the young boy became in the far country trying to find life without the father! Someone has said, "Trying to find life without God is like taking heat out of fire, melody out of music, taste out of food, water out of the river, and clouds from the sky. It is like trying to come out of the wilderness without a map and attempting to find our way in the darkness without light."

Without God, we are like a leaf cut off from a limb.

Another mistake of the young boy was that he forgot the source of his strength. He thought he was able to control his behavior. He never dreamed when he left home that he would end up in the pig pen. No boy or girl would want to end up in a pig pin, but it's happened again and again.

Whenever we forget that the Lord is the source of our strength, we find ourselves giving into the lower self, taking the low road rather than the high road.

We need God for the source of our strength. Without Him, we weaken, falter and we fall into life's gutters, wretched.

It is so easy to forget who we are, living like beasts, satisfying only lust. God has made us after His image—as persons.

Our souls are never satisfied until they rest in God. Wretched, hungry, without money or friends, beaten, helpless, the boy came to his senses and recognized that he could not make it on his own, that he needed the father. There is no real life outside the Father, God. Likewise, he recognized that he was not a beast, but a son.

He came to his senses and said, "I will go back to my father." It is a touch of beauty to see a person bounce back. It is deeply moving to see a defeated person bounce back, to see a person make a turn for the better, to see a person who has hit rock bottom move upward.

They used to call it conversion, new birth—being born again. The wonderful thing is that it can happen. A miracle in the heart can happen. I have seen it happen!

I have known it to happen within me! Through the grace of God in Christ, people can be changed. Weak persons can be made strong. Bad persons can be made good. Wicked persons can be made righteous. Sinful persons through grace can be saved. God is able, willing, and ready.

> Come, ye sinners, poor and needy,
> Sick and wounded by the fall—
> Jesus stands ready to help you—
> full of pity, love, and power.
> —Joseph Hart

WHEN WINNING IS LOSING

> Then said Jesus unto his disciples, If any man will come
> after me, let him deny himself, and take up his cross, and
> follow me. For whosoever will save his life shall lose it; and
> whosoever will lose his life for my sake shall find it. For
> what is a man profited, if he shall gain the whole world, and
> lose his own soul? Or what shall a man give in exchange for
> his soul?
>
> —Matt. 16:24-26 KJV

There is a terrible notion prevailing in our world today that winning
is everything, that nothing is more important than winning. "Win the
game!" coaches say to their teams. "Win the contest!" contestants are
told by their sponsors. "Win the election!" members of political parties
say to candidates.

What a mess we are in today as a nation because of this notion that
winning is everything—and because we perceive it to be everything.
We must win at any expenses.

It is likely that many candidates who win in the election Tuesday
will be the real losers. They may get elected to office but will have lost
something far more vital—their souls.

Winners are losers when they resort to evil to win. Whenever a
person says things or does things that he or she really doesn't believe in
to win any contest, he or she loses more than he or she gains. Whenever
a person damages the character of an opponent to defeat him or her,
he or she loses more than he or she gains. Whenever a person cheats to
win any contest, he or she loses more than he or she gains. Whenever
money rather than ability gets a person an office or an advancement, he
or she loses more than he or she gains. Whenever a person is deceptive
to get ahead, he or she loses more than he or she gains. Whenever a

person lies (and oh, what lying we have had in recent weeks) to get elected, he or she loses more than he or she gains.

In our text, Jesus presents a great challenge to His disciples. It is a constant theme in His teachings. Again and again, the Master confronted them with the challenge of the Christian life.

He said that first you must deny yourself. You must learn in every moment of life to say no to self and yes to God and to make God the ruling principle, the ruling passion of life. That means assent to God. "Take my life, God, and use it as you will."

Jesus also said to His disciples, "You must take up your cross."

We must sacrifice time and pleasure in order to serve God through others. It may mean that we will have to give up personal ambition to serve Christ. Even if we are convinced that He is leading us somewhere where the reward appears small, we must go.

The Christian life represents a life of sacrifice. Our Lord challenges us to sacrifice daily to serve Him through serving others. "Let him take up his cross daily," Christ said.

When we sacrifice to serve Him (through serving others), our Lord taught, we find life. Persons can exist without sacrificing to serve others, but life never comes alive. To simply have lungs breathing and a heart beating is existence, but not life. To be alive is to have peace in the soul and joy in the heart.

The person who plays life safe—refusing to risk life for Christ's sake, for the cause of right, for the advancement of the kingdom—will lose real life.

If we are constantly searching for safety, security, ease, and comfort, we are losing the satisfying life.

If every decision we make is in our interest alone, we are losing the meaning of life.

If life becomes a selfish thing for us, we lose the radiance of life.

If life is spent attempting to always come out on top, we lose in time the zest of living.

If life becomes an earthbound thing, we fail to reach for the stars.

If life is centered on always winning, we lose our souls, for we will sacrifice those moral principles that make us real persons to win.

Charlemagne (Charles the Great), emperor of the Holy Roman Empire in the ninth century—noted for stimulating interest in education, philosophy, and literature, and for strengthening the church—was buried with an open Bible on his knee with a finger pointing to the words: "For what is a man profited, if he gains the whole world and loses his own soul?"

"What does it profit," Jesus asked, "if we gain the whole world at the expense of losing the soul, the person?" Winning the praise of the world—the praise of men—and losing the praise of God? Winning earthly glory, but losing heavenly glory?

It's a poor exchange to gain what is temporary for what is permanent, to gain the world and lose real life in this world and in the next.

It's a poor exchange to give up the way of Jesus for the way of the world. He bids Christians to follow Him! "I am the way to life!"

A SAINT GOES HOME

In Psalm 116:15 KJV, we read the words: "Precious in the sight of the Lord is the death of his saints."

Death is not generally looked upon as precious. It is something that brings sorrow and tears. Within most of us is the fear of death and dying. We wish we could escape it. The late Vernon Johns recalled a person who once said that if he knew where he was supposed to die, he would move to another city. We can move but cannot run from death. The place cannot be known, nor the time, nor the circumstance. But one thing is certain: death will come.

Death is not a desirable thing for most people. It means separation from those we love. It is not a desirable thing to a physician. For him, it is defeat. It means that medical science with all of its advancement cannot stem the tide of death. Science has been successful in prolonging life, but not in eliminating death. It never will.

Death is not a desirable thing to members of the family of the deceased, who must be left alone. It is an extremely painful when the deceased is one on whom the family primarily depends.

The text does not suggest that death is a desirable thing to the family or to the physician.

Regardless of the faith of the family and its knowledge that a loved one has gone to be with the Lord, the loss in separation is great and painful.

The text says, "Precious in the sight of the Lord is the death of his saints."

Death is a precious thing to God only in the lives of certain people—saints. When God completes his molding of the life of a person and the person is a beautiful soul, it becomes a precious moment for God. It means the work of the person designed by God has been completed.

How thrilling, how fulfilling, how satisfying, how great it is when a person completes an assignment! God assigns all of us work to do. How precious is that moment when we can say, "I've done my work; I've sung my song."

Death is precious in the sight of the Lord—for those who have completed their assignments. We are fitted for eternity when the process of molding and remaking has been completed and we have done our work for God.

The saint completes the work assigned to him or her. And when that is done, God sends an angel of death to call the soul home unto Himself. Precious was death to a saint who had done her work and had sung her song and was going to be with her Lord forever and forever.

HOW LIFE IS MEASURED

Life is never measured by how many years we live, but by the kindly things we do and the happiness we give to others.

We come together this afternoon to pay tribute to one whose life did not reach the three score years and ten the psalmist talks about in the ninetieth Psalm, but who got the best of the years God granted him to live.

New American Standard translates the psalmist's words found in the twelfth verse: "Teach us to number our days and recognize how few they are; help us to make the best use of them." This is what God, our maker, calls on all of us to do—to get the best of life granted to us. The mature person and the wise person seeks to make every day count. Ultimately, God will not measure our lives in terms of quantity, but in terms of quality; not in terms of what we acquired for ourselves, but what we gave to others; not the happiness we achieved, but the happiness we gave to others.

The most important relationship we establish is the one with the creator and sustainer of life. We never get the best of life unless our lives are linked with His. We can never bring our sinful wills and our restless souls under control without God. Without Him, we drift to and fro through life like a ship without a sail. In fact, without Him, we can live our three score years and ten and really never live. He is not only our maker, but He is the sustainer. Without Him, we are cut off from the source and supplier of life, as a tree cut off from the root.

He was a diligent seeker of the good life and sought it where it could be found. He sought the Lord through studying the eternal Word and regularly worshiping with God's people in God's house. He found Him and learned to love Him.

He grew in knowledge and grace of our Lord so that he was prepared to die. Sensible people prepare to die. They recognize the fact that we are pilgrims traveling in a strange world. We should not become so contented in this world that we forget where home is. Death should not be a surprise to us. We make the best of each day because we don't know when death will overtake us.

We should seek to be at peace with God and our fellow travelers each day. When we are peace with our Lord and our fellow men, we can die peacefully.

THE PEACEFUL LIFE

One of the most sought-after things in life is peace. We deeply yearn for a peaceful life. It escapes most of us because we turn outward seeking it.

Peace cannot be achieved by trying to control what happens to us from the outside. We cannot shield ourselves from all of the bad things that happen to us.

The storms of life rage, and we find ourselves helpless against them. We are not in control of outward forces that threaten the peaceful life.

We cannot always protect ourselves from enemies. They attack us from behind and strike us at night.

The wind blows into our lives and we find ourselves without outer shelter.

The clouds rise when things are going well with us, and we don't have the power to let the sunshine through.

Disease invades these frail and feeble bodies, and even the best earthly physicians find their knowledge and skill insufficient to deal with our sickness.

We stand baffled and helpless by the bedsides of those who are very dear to us—unable to do or say anything to ease their unbearable pain.

With all of the outward adversities that come to us in life, you ask, "How can we have a peaceful life?" Is there a peace that can abide when things go wrong?

The answer is yes. We can turn to Him who can bring inward peace in spite of the outward storms that wildly rage in our lives.

That kind of peace, however, can never be acquired through our efforts. It is a peace that is a gift from God.

The apostle Paul speaks of it in Philippians 4:7 RSV: "the peace of God which passes all understanding." It is a paradox. With our limited reasoning power, it doesn't make sense.

We all understand the peace that comes when suffering is relieved or the burden is taken away.

But the peace of God is a peace that comes when the wind keeps on blowing in our lives, when adversities mount rather than vanish.

It is the peace that comes when in our hunger food is not forthcoming; when in our loneliness, we don't find a friend.

It is the peace that comes when our sickness is not healed, and the dark night of physical suffering becomes darker.

It is the peace that comes when the doctors and nurses have done all that they can do and walk out on us.

It is the peace that comes when the minister at the graveside says, "Earth to earth, ashes to ashes, dust to dust."

It is the peace that she came to know in her struggles with the adversities of life, on her sickbed in agony, and even when she came to die.

It is the peace that she constantly sang about—"Peace in the Valley."

There is inward peace in the valley when we come to know the peace of God.

PART IV

SELECTED EDITORIALS, WRITINGS, AND SPEECHES

EXPANDING OUR SENSE OF THANKFULNESS

(Editorial by the Rev. Otis L. Hairston Sr. published in the *Greensboro Record* on November 25, 1982)

Thanksgiving 1982 finds our nation in a state of despair, bitterness, frustration, and fear. Fraught with increased unemployment, racial, economic, and international strife, and coupled with hunger, crime, and a loss of a sense of human worth by the oppressed, the climate in our nation is indeed unhealthy.

Millions in our country will find it extremely difficult to lift their voices in praises in the midst of deprivation. Especially will this be true with those who are poignantly aware of the fact that they are not responsible for their predicament.

On the other hand, millions who enjoy the bounty of the earth will likewise fail to lift their voices in praise. They mistakenly believe that they deserve what they have. Some even feel that they themselves have produced their bounty through their wisdom, skill, and hard work.

Regardless of our plight, all of us need to expand our sense of gratefulness. The great missing note in our generation is the missing note of thankfulness. There needs to be cultivated a sense of gratitude on the human level. All of us need to recognize and appreciate the role that family, friends, and even foes play in our successes and in our general well-being.

Thanksgiving ought to be a time when we pause long enough to remember the little but necessary deeds that others do for us. It ought to lead to and reinforce the practice of expressing thanks to persons who perform even so-called insignificant deeds of kindness for us. The practice ought to be cultivated to the point that it becomes a habitual custom in our lives.

Even more important is the need for all of us to expand our sense of thankfulness to Him "from whom all blessings flow." We need to remember the spirit of the Pilgrim fathers. In 1623, they paused to give thanks to God not because they had so much, but because they recognized that God had brought them safely through drought, starvation, and death.

Furthermore, we need to remember that President Abraham Lincoln issued the first general Thanksgiving proclamation on October 3, 1863, during the darkest days of the Civil War. A statement of his should be meditated upon by our generation:

> I fear that we have forgotten the gracious Hand which has preserved us in peace, and multiplied, enriched, and strengthened us, and have vainly imagined in the deceitfulness of our hearts that all these blessings were produced by some superior wisdom and virtue of our own. Intoxicated with unbroken success, we have become too self-sufficient to feel the necessity of the redeeming and preserving grace, too proud to pray to God who made it.

Thanksgiving is a season to recognize anew the blessings of a kind and gracious God and to cultivate a sense of daily gratefulness. We need to learn to thank God for the common blessings of life so often overlooked—the air to breathe, the water to drink, and the food to eat. We need to thank Him for the beauty of the earth, sky, and sea, and for the melodious music of birds, the sound of which lifts our spirits. We need to thank Him for families to support us and friends with whom we share our joys and sorrows.

Like the apostle Paul, we need to expand our sense of thankfulness so that we can "give thanks in all circumstances." Even if we are not able to give thanks for all things, we can give thanks in all things. Like the psalmist, we need to expand our sense of thankfulness to reach the divine level when we can say: "I desire to do your will, O my God (Ps. 40:8 NIV).

Like St. Francis of Assisi, we need to expand our sense of thankfulness so that our blessings from God become not an end but a means to an end, enabling us to pray as he did, "Lord, make me an instrument of Thy peace. Where there is hatred, let me show love; where there is injury, pardon; where there is doubt, faith; where there is despair, hope; where there is sadness, joy; where there is darkness, light."

CHRISTMAS OUT OF FOCUS

(Article written for the *Greensboro Record* as part of a weekly feature run in cooperation with the Greensboro Ministerial Fellowship)

Are you ready for Christmas? is the common and constant question asked following Thanksgiving and leading up to Christmas Day.

The question itself implies that extensive preparation is needed to get ready. Millions spend many hours shopping for suitable gifts for relatives and friends, securing and addressing Christmas cards, decorating yards, doors and windows, planning dinners and parties attempting to get ready for Christmas. These are the kinds of things most people conceive as being essential in order to get ready for Christmas.

In our commercial society, Advent, the season of preparation for the coming of God, is seldom observed. Material preparation for Christmas is foremost in the minds of most of us. Things have become the mountain in our lives, and personhood a molehill. We have gone so haywire with our buying, our eating, and our outward display that we have lost sight of what Christmas means. We forget that it is a birthday of a king who was meek and lowly, born in a stable, and wrapped in swaddling clothes. He showed us what real personhood is.

The prophet Isaiah, almost a thousand years before God unfolded his love through human flesh, proclaimed: "In the wilderness, Prepare ye the way of the Lord, make straight in the desert a highway for our God" (Isa. 40:3 KJV).

John the Baptist echoed the voice of the prophet just before the public ministry of Jesus: "Prepare ye the way of the Lord."

Getting ready for Christmas really means preparing the way for the Lord, making room in our lives for the Christ child. It is getting the spirit of Him who is meek and lowly. It is turning from ourselves and helping to take care of the needs of others. To truly celebrate Christmas, the light must not only be around us but within us.

Phillips Brooks, a great preacher of another century, expressed what ought to be the prayer of those who seek to get ready for the real Christmas.

> Holy Child of Bethlehem: descend to us, we pray;
> Cast out our sin, and enter in, be born in us today.
> We hear the Christmas angels the great glad tidings tell;
> O come to us, abide with us, our Lord Immanuel.

TO THE PASTOR

(Sermon given at the installation of a pastor)

The greatest thing you can do as pastor is to help produce members who will reflect Jesus Christ in their lives in the church and outside the church.

The ultimate aim of our preaching, teaching, and living should be to produce better people (saints).

The church must do more than get members to be religious. It must get people to be righteous. Members can be religious and raise hell in the church. Some of the most religious members I know are the biggest troublemakers in the church. They work just as hard to tear down the church as others work to build up the church.

In his first letter to the church of Corinth, the apostle Paul gives some advice to a church filled with strife and divided into factions. The situation in the Corinthian church was so complex and many-sided that he had to follow the first letter with a second letter.

In the third chapter, he speaks to them as infants in Christ. The envy and strife among them were evidence that they were babies in the Christian faith. Their behavior was not becoming mature Christians. There were those who bragged about Paul and glorified him, and there were others who were in Apollos's corner and glorified him as their spiritual teacher. Paul condemns their folly by saying that Apollos was nothing but a servant of God and that he [Paul] was nothing but a servant of God. They were only fellow workers and both belonged to God. Those who were split into factions were only troublemakers. They could be officers of the church, but were not persons of God.

Then Paul had to confront a division in the church over the argument about the superiority of gifts (twelfth chapter). There developed disunity among church members over which gifts were more important than others. All of the gifts—wisdom, knowledge, faith, healing, prophecy, speaking in tongues, the power to interpret tongues—come from the same God who causes them in every person.

The church is the body of Christ. Just as every part of the human body is important and performs its function for the good of the whole, so every member's differing gifts are designed for the glory of the church for Christ.

Paul follows the twelfth chapter with a discussion of the gift that excels all gifts—love, the way to unity.

Persons in the church can speak with tongues like angels, but if they have not love, they are only clanging cymbals, making a lot of noise. They can have the gift of prophecy, understand all sacred secrets, and have all knowledge; they may have all faith so that mountains can be moved, but if they have not love, they are nothing. They give all that they have to the poor, and surrender their bodies to be burned, but if they have not love, it is no good, and amounts to nothing at all.

In the sixteenth chapter, Paul appeals to the members of the church at Corinth to hold fast to the faith. Don't treat service in the church casually. Don't be easygoing with God's work. Be vigorous, be courageous, and be faithful.

Paul summons Timothy—his son in the ministry, a young man—to come to Corinth to join in ministering. In 1 Corinthians 16:10 LBV, Paul says, "If Timothy comes make him feel at home, for he is doing the Lord's work just as I am."

The greatest thing that members can do for a new pastor is to put him at ease. See that he has nothing to fear as your minister! Make him feel at home, that he is among friends. Let him serve without pressure! It is a terrible thing for a minister of the gospel of Christ to serve under pressure. He cannot do his best if he works under pressure. He needs to know that he has the unqualified support of his boards, other officers, and members.

The conditions that existed in the church at Corinth, keeping ministers from being at ease, should not exist in any church today. There ought not to be factions, groups clamoring to excel and be more important than others. Every group is or should play a vital part in making the church all that Christ wants it to be.

There should be no strife because some officers or members think more highly of themselves than they ought to think. Every member ought to be looked upon as someone special in the life of the church whether he or she has ten talents, five talents, or one talent. The church ought not to be divided by classes in terms of education, social, or economic standards.

The love described by the apostle in the thirteenth chapter of his first letter to Corinthians should, with the grace of God, be practiced. Love is patient and kind, never jealous, never boastful, never selfish or rude. (Love has good manners.) Love does not demand its own way. It is not irritable or touchy. It does not hold grudges and will hardly even notice when others do it wrong. It rejoices not in the failures of others, but in the successes.

In the Baptist Church covenant, we pledge "to walk together in Christian love, to strive for the advancement of this church in knowledge, and holiness, to give it a place in our affections, prayers, and services."

We also pledge to watch over, to pray for, to exhort, and stir up each other unto every good word, and work to guard each other's reputations, not needlessly exposing the infirmities of others.

Love is the way to unity in the church; Christian love is the way to avoid strife in the church; Christian love is the way to prevent factions in the church. Practicing Christian love is the way to put at ease the pastor of the church.

The essential reason the pastor ought to be at ease is that he is doing the work of the Lord.

Paul pleads with the church to put Timothy at ease not primarily for his own sake, but for the work he will do. He should be respected because he is the servant of Christ.

It is not the pastor who glorifies the work; it is the work that glorifies the pastor. The pastor is a worker for the Lord. He serves people, but is a worker for the Lord. His real boss is not his board, but the One who called him into service and the One to whom he will ultimately have to answer. The pastor should not lose sight of the One for whom he is working.

I visited a young minister in the hospital. He had suffered a mental breakdown because of the pressures brought about by the disgruntled members of his Methodist church. He sought to do the right thing—to preach the truth as God led him—regardless of the verdict of members.

He was looked down upon because he was doing too much afflicting and not comforting. The pastor must comfort, but he also must afflict those who are too comfortable in their sin.

I said to him that the important thing is to not forget who you are working for. We cannot work for God unless we condemn wrong in high places and low places. He has called us to work for Him and to proclaim His Word without respect to persons.

Finally, preach the Word with courage and conviction; that Word which is the gospel of grace but also the gospel of judgment; that Word which comforts the afflicted and also afflicts the comfortable; that Word which the forces cannot destroy and time cannot erase. Preach the Word and never lose confidence that it is the power unto salvation.

It is food for the hungry; it is water for the thirsty; it is clothing for the naked; it is a friend for the friendless; it is hope for the hopeless; it is a physician for the sick and eternal life for the dying.

Preach that Word.

For it will make bad persons good, and good persons better. It will lift the fallen; it will strengthen the weak. It will bring home the prodigals. It will set the prisoners free!

Preach that Word.

Preach it with all of the power of your mind, body, and soul. Preach it even if you are persecuted and persons turn their backs on you! Preach in season and out of season!

Preach it until your tongue is paralyzed in death and the great Master of the universe will say, "Well done!"

You can say with great satisfaction like the apostle Paul when you come to the end, "I have fought a good fight, I have finished my course, I have kept the faith . . . for me a crown of righteousness, which the Lord, the righteous judge, shall give me" (2 Tim. 4:8 KJV).

Through many dangers, toils and snares
I have already come;
T'was grace [God's grace in Christ] that brought me safe thus far,
And grace [God's grace] will lead me home.
—John Newton

A PROFILE OF THE
CHRISTIAN MINISTER

(Given on the anniversary of a pastor)

Never has there been a period in history when the need for ministers to set an example of true Christian living has been greater. We have preachers springing up from everywhere today. This past Friday, a thirty-year-old man approached me about offering him instruction for preaching. He wanted to be a preacher and get him a church. A minister had told him that the only thing he needed was to learn how to preach, and it would require only about two months if he found the right teacher. His concern was to be able to stand before a congregation and give an acceptable sermon.

My response to him was that the ministry is different from any other profession. The doctor chooses medicine; the lawyer chooses law; the teacher chooses teaching, but the minister is chosen. He enters the ministry because there is, in one sense, no other choice. God moves on the minds and hearts of those who are called ministers in such a way that they have no other choice. I also said to him that the Christian minister not only preaches the gospel of Christ, but he or she puts the gospel in action in his or her daily life. He or she tries not only to tell people how to live the Christian life, but through the grace of God, he or she shows them.

We pay tribute today to a minister who not only preaches about the Christ like way but who strives to live it. The Christian minister is one who seeks to do in his life what he can never effectively do through his preaching or teaching. The Christian minister has something sacred on the inside that shows on the outside. It is seen in his walk. It is seen in his talk. It is seen in the manner in which he looks at people. He has had a firsthand experience with Christ the Lord and has that saving power within which comes from that experience.

The new birth in Christ is the beginning and end of preaching. The story of salvation must be told by one who knows it, not by one who has merely heard about it. The great preachers are the Christian ministers who know Christ the Lord firsthand. Their preaching is to get people to get a taste of the redeeming love of God in Christ.

In the thirteenth chapter of first Corinthians, the apostle paints a picture of Jesus as he lifts love as the supreme gift. Jesus can be substituted where love is used in that great chapter. It is a description of Jesus. In concluding the chapter, Paul lists the three greatest gifts that a Christian can possess: "so faith, hope, and love abide, these three, but the greatest of these is love" (1 Cor. 13:13 RSV).

The Christian minister possesses these three qualities, which he or she attempts to pass on to those in his or her congregation. He has not only lifted these great qualities of the Christian life to you in his preaching and in his teaching, but through his life.

He has shown you a faith strong enough for the darkness. There have been difficult moments, trying times during his years. No minister serves a church many years without facing dark days. Dark days test our faith in God. God does not send dark days in the life of a church. Members bring them on through their failure to let Christ be Lord. We push His way of love aside and seek to have our way. We become selfish and mean and get the church in an uproar. The Christian minister, faced with the raging storms, maintains his faith in God. He is convinced the Lord is going to work it out. When the ship confronts the troubling waters, the Christian minster has the faith of the apostle Paul who declared when a ship was shipwrecked and in danger of sinking and the crew fearful, "So keep up your courage, men, for I have faith in God" (Acts 27:25 NIV). He has shown you faith when the ship was in danger.

He has not only shown in his ministry a faith that is unshakable, but the second great quality—that of hope. When the way has seemed unclear at times, he has managed to keep hope alive. When at the bedside of patients, when things did not look good, and the odds were not favorable, he has said to anxious family members, "Let's have hope. God is able."

The Christian minister is one who makes love his greatest aim. Love is the one gift that denotes discipleship. The greatest attribute of God is not power but love. The Christian patterns his or her life after God by loving. No minister can be Christ like without the capacity to love people. He cannot teach love and preach love without living it. He has sought to love with the God-type love expressed in terms of caring and sharing.

SERMON GIVEN ON THE TWENTY-FIFTH ANNIVERSARY OF A PASTOR

> It was he [Christ] who gave some to be apostles, some to be prophets, some to be evangelists, and some to be pastors and teachers.
>
> —Eph. 4:11 NIV

The word *pastor* in Ephesians is the Latin word for *shepherd*.

We have failed in our day to look upon the pastor as primarily a shepherd. Many pastors fail to view themselves as shepherds. They conceive themselves as preachers, as evangelists, as prophets, as teachers.

The concept of pastors as shepherds is lifted in the Old Testament and in the New Testament.

Jesus in John 10 is portrayed as the Good Shepherd. He is the shepherd who will risk his life to seek and to save one straying sheep. There is no better loved picture of Jesus than the Good Shepherd. It is a picture that paints the patience and the love of God. In the Old Testament, there is a given contrast between the good and the bad, the faithful and the unfaithful shepherd, the real shepherd and the false shepherd.

A real shepherd was born to his task. He was sent out with the flock as soon as he was old enough to go; the sheep became his friends and his companions, and it became second nature to think of them before he thought of himself. But the false shepherd came into the job, not as a calling, but as a means of making money. He was in it simply and solely for the pay he could get. He had no sense of responsibility. He was a hireling.

The good shepherd, the real shepherd, was one who cared for the sheep and would risk his life to see that they were protected and nourished.

His life was not easy. He was never off duty. There being little grass, the sheep were bound to wander, and since there were no protecting walls, the sheep had to be constantly watched.

He had to guard the sheep against wild animals, and there were always thieves and robbers ready to steal the sheep. The shepherd was sleepless, weather-beaten, leaning on his staff, and looking out over the scattered sheep, every one of them on his heart.

He had patient love for his flock. The prophet Jeremiah warned the unfaithful shepherd, "Woe to the shepherds who are destroying and scattering the sheep of my pasture!" (Jer. 23:1 NIV).

The prophet Ezekiel indicted the false leaders who seek their own good rather than the good of the flock.

The faithful shepherd shows the patient love of God. He keeps a constant watch over all the sheep and will sacrifice to see that they are cared for.

For twenty-five years you have had a faithful shepherd who has watched over the flock here.

He has been a real shepherd. He has not thought primarily of what the church would do for him, but what he could do for the church. He cared more about members than about himself.

He has not looked upon his calling to the ministry as a means of making money, but as a means of faithfully tending God's flock.

He has not found it easy. He has had sleepless nights tending the flock—visiting hospitals, being with families during critical sickness, and when death invaded families.

He has been weather-beaten and drained at times, but through the grace of God, has been faithful in tending the flock. He has guarded the sheep.

He has recognized that God called him not only to preach to the church and to teach the church, but to care for its members, to love all of them, to set an example for them.

For twenty-five years, he has done this. God has been glorified and magnified; you have been blessed.

Keep on tending the sheep.

CHURCH MISSION

Ministries with Other Races

(Presented to the Statewide Baptist Missions Conference,
Green Street Baptist Church, High Point, North Carolina,
February 25, 1972)

One of the extremely difficult frontiers for the American church to cross is that of Christian ministries with other races. This is especially true with white churches in regards to blacks.

Since the antebellum era, white churches have ministered to black people. However, the ministry has for the most part been motivated by selfish interest.

In 1835, the Virginia Baptist General Association adopted a plan for instruction to "our colored population who are in a deplorable state of ignorance." The report affirmed that "religious instruction makes them more faithful and obedient slaves."

White churches in the present era often are anxious to minister to blacks or to participate in joint projects as a means of "show pieces." Like "show windows" displaying articles that are not available inside, the ministries of churches often are "show pieces." Deep within, there is deep-seated racism. Where there is racism, there is not Christian love. Ministries are not Christian when love is not the motivating force.

Blacks today are hesitant about being ministered to by whites or becoming involved in joint mission ventures with whites because of their failure to recognize blacks as equals. The faith is affirmed that all men are created in the image of God, but there is a failure on the part of white Christians to accept the equality of blacks. Dr. H. Shelton Smith, former Duke Divinity School professor, says white Christians say "in the image of God" but

White American Christian can say "one nation under God with liberty and justice for all," and at the same time devote their minds and material resources to see that two communities are maintained. They can oppose busing of school pupils, and at the same time fight open housing. They can sing the lyrics of the hymn writer John Oxenham:

In Christ there is no east or west,
In Him no south or north,
But one great fellowship of love
Throughout the whole wide earth.

And then treat blacks as "things" to be manipulated.

They can cry for law and order and like Governor Wallace encourage citizens to disregard Supreme Court orders.

Following civil rights gains in the sixties, blacks were hopeful that the church would cross the difficult frontier of Christian ministries with other races. It was hoped by many black Christians that American churches would not go grudgingly, as Jonah went, but lovingly and unitedly "to preach good tidings to the humble . . . to proclaim liberty to the captives, and the opening of the prison to those who are bound" (Isa. 61:1 MLB).

Christ still calls His church not only to go to all peoples everywhere and make them His disciples and to baptize them in the name of the Father and of the Son, and of the Holy Spirit, but also to teach them to obey everything He commanded.

The great commandments are, of course, love God and love neighbor.

KEEP KING'S DREAM ALIVE

(Guest column for the Greensboro *News & Record*
published January 20, 1986)

A national holiday honoring one of the most eminent leaders produced by America is not only fitting, but will no doubt be extremely fruitful for a nation that is still divided by race, class, community, and religion.

To celebrate nationwide the life and work of one who was a descendant of the slave system but who gave the greatest projection of the American dream ever set forth will "lift the legacy" to the level it rightly deserves. To hear the voice of Martin Luther King Jr. resounding throughout this nation today—the dream of "a beautiful America"—will prick the consciences of millions of Americans who proudly recite "one nation under God with liberty and justice for all," but who vote and work against fulfilling the creed.

It is impossible to estimate fully the impact of Dr. King during his brief life on earth, but it is highly possible that no person in the history of this nation was more widely heard and had greater influence in mobilizing people to become active in working to rid this nation of racism, sexism, economic injustice, violence, and war.

It is certain that he was the leading exponent of nonviolence in days when violence was rampant. Our nation was undoubtedly saved from many bloodbaths during the sixties (and even today) because of his teaching and persistence that nonviolence be used as a tactic in the struggle for freedom and justice. Even those who disliked him recognized that he symbolized the best in humanity in insisting that love, rather than hate, be the approach in dealing with violence.

On this historic day in our nation, as we celebrate the life and dream of Martin Luther King, all Americans should pause to reflect on the dream he projected in his most famous speech, "I Have a Dream." It is essential that the hope for "a beautiful America" be kept alive. In this day when despair is prevalent among so many Americans, it is important that the dream be echoed.

The vision of this great prophet "that one day this nation will rise up and live out the true meaning of its creed, 'We hold these truths to be self-evident, that all men are created equal,'" must be kept alive. It must be kept alive as a means of inspiring those who will shape tomorrow's world to commit themselves to fulfill the dream. The dream must be kept alive to lead more of us to become "drum majors for justice and peace" in these days of complacency. The dream must be kept alive so that one day enough people in enough places will rise up and bring in the day of brotherhood and end the night of wrong.

SPEECH TO THE CRESCENT ROTARY CLUB HONORING DR. MARTIN LUTHER KING JR.

January 15, 1996

Permit me to salute you for devoting the meeting today to honor Dr. Martin Luther King Jr. I am extremely grateful for the kind invitation extended to me for the club by my longtime friend, Owen Lewis.

I was privileged to hear Dr. King speak in 1957 and again in 1958 while residing in Raleigh. I was in Chicago in 1966 studying at the Urban Training Center when King was leading a campaign against slum housing and a campaign to integrate housing. He had a close call May 16, 1966, when he was stoned while leading a march through Chicago in connection with the campaign. I was in Washington and a part of the historic march on Washington, August 28, 1963, when he delivered the famous "I Have a Dream" speech. The speech has been heralded as his greatest speech, and one of the truly great speeches in American history.

"God moves in a mysterious way, his wonders to perform," in the words of a hymn by William Cowper The refusal of Rosa Parks on December 1, 1955, to move to the back of a bus in Birmingham led to a movement that changed many aspects of American history, and the emerging of a leader who became a modern Moses.

A grandson of a former slave gave America a new birth of freedom through nonviolence. America's birth was through violence, but the new birth of freedom was through nonviolence.

It is fitting for our nation to have Martin Luther King Jr. inducted into the most exclusive of all American clubs. Only one other American, President George Washington, is honored by a national holiday.

Perhaps no American has had a greater or more positive impact upon the nation than this grandson of a former slave.

In the signing ceremony in the Rose Garden of the White House, November 2, 1983, making King's birthday a national holiday, President Ronald Reagan made the following statement:

> When I was thinking of the contribution to our country, the man that we're honoring today, a passage attributed to the American poet John Greenleaf Whittier comes to mind: "Each crisis brings its word and deed." In America, in the fifties and sixties, one of the important crises we faced was racial discrimination. The man whose words and deed in that crisis stirred our nation to the very depths of its soul was Dr. Martin Luther King Jr.
>
> Now our nation has decided to honor Dr. Martin Luther King Jr. by setting aside a day each year to remember him and the just cause he stood for. We've made historic strides since Rosa Parks refused to go to the back of a bus.
>
> As a democratic people, we can take pride in the knowledge that we Americans recognized a grave injustice and took action to correct it, and should remember that in far too many countries, people like Dr. King never had the opportunity to speak out at all.
>
> But traces of bigotry still mar America. So each year on Martin Luther King Day, let us not only recall Dr. King, but rededicate ourselves to the commandments he believed in and sought every day. "Thou shalt love thy God with all thy heart and they neighbor as thyself." And I just have to believe that if all of us, young and old, Republicans and Democrats, do all we can to live up to the commandments, then we will see the day when Dr. King's dream comes true, and in his words, "All of God's children will be able to say with new meaning, 'land where my fathers died, land of the pilgrim's pride, from every mountainside, let freedom ring.'"

Since the setting aside of a national holiday honoring Dr. King, many persons have asked, "Why should King be placed above other

American leader who has had a great impact in making America a just and good nation?"

I would respond to the question by saying that not only did the words and deeds of Martin Luther give a new birth of freedom, but it was achieved without violence. The nonviolence approach to overcome evil practices was lifted to a new and noble level.

Dr. King was fully committed to nonviolence. Nonviolence was a principal factor making Dr. King a leader among leaders. Echoing through all of King's work is a sense of passionate commitment to tearing down the walls of oppression through nonviolent means.

King was a nonviolent liberator. In spite of criticism from foes and friends, he disapproved of America's involvement in the Vietnam War.

He disapproved of America's treatment of the poor because he perceived poverty as violence. To permit people to die because of hunger, poor and no housing or health care is violent.

King not only taught nonviolence, but he lived it. He insisted—really, he demanded—that those involved in the freedom movement not resort to the practice of an eye for an eye. It would result in both parties being blind.

His conviction was that noble goals should be achieved by noble means.

In his "I Have a Dream" speech, Dr. King sought to set the right tone for protesting against wrongs: "In the process of gaining our rightful place, we must not be guilty of wrongful deeds. Let us not seek to satisfy our thirst for freedom by drinking from the cup of bitterness and hatred. We must forever conduct our struggle on the high plain of dignity and discipline. We must not allow our creative protest to degenerate into physical violence."

King sought to promote that new dimension of love commanded by Christ when He said, "Love your enemies, and pray for anyone who mistreats you." Wish good for those who mistreat you. In the words of the apostle Paul, "Overcome evil with good."

The challenge for America and for us today is to keep alive the nonviolent approach in dealing with evil forces and to keep hope alive (in the words of Jesse Jackson).

There is something in this universe that justifies Thomas Carlyle in saying, "No lie can live forever."

There is something in this universe that justifies William Cullen Bryant in saying, "Truth crushed to the earth will rise again."

There is something in this universe that justifies James Russell Lowell in saying,

> Truth forever on the scaffold
> Wrong forever on the throne,
> Yet that scaffold sways the future
> And being the dim unknown stands God
> Within the shadows keeping watch above His own.

Let's keep the dream alive!

I am not completely pleased with what is happening in our nation and in our community today—poverty that contributes to an increase in crime, the poor becoming poorer, and the rich becoming richer, growing greed, the clamor to balance the economic budget without a creative and sincere effort to balance the moral budget, corruption in low places and in high places—but I still hold to the dream. I still have hope that one day enough leaders and enough ordinary people in enough places will rise up and bring in the day of brotherhood and end the night of wrong.

Let us keep hope alive!

SEGREGATION

(Article by the Rev. Otis L. Hairston Sr., March 2, 1956)

Recent court decisions relating to segregation because of race in the use of public facilities have created real problems for many communities in the southern region of our country. We are not realistic when we fail to look upon the transition from a segregated school system to a desegregated system in North Carolina as being difficult.

The fact that such a change is complicated does not excuse us, however, from moving forward. Each community is responsible for preparing its citizens for a program of compliance. Under the pupil assignment law, the state has shifted the responsibility to the local community. The governor's plan of voluntary separate school attendance has not worked, and it will not work as evidenced by court cases in which Negro pupils are seeking, through their parents, entrance into the nearest schools in their communities.

If we recognize that the Supreme Court has spoken definitely and finally on enforced segregation, and that those who have been exploited are fearlessly requesting an end to the practice of segregation, then we must conclude that there is no way of evading eventual desegregation.

In the light of this, the community should not spend its time, energy, and money trying to get around the inevitable, but should dedicate its efforts and resources to preparing the children, parents, teachers, and other citizens for the transition.

Channels of communication should be established between parents, teachers, and citizens in general to work out this most difficult problem in a spirit of understanding.

We must not fight against the wind through a program of evasion. E. Stanley Jones has well said that "He who spits against the wind spits in his own face."

WHY BUS?

(Written by the Rev. Otis L. Hairston Sr. while a member of the Greensboro Board of Education)

On July 27, 1967, President Lyndon B. Johnson addressed the nation after several weeks of grave violence in many of the major cities of America. Violence on a wide scale had also taken place during the previous two summers.

The opening statement of the address indicated the seriousness of the disorder.

"We have endured a week such as no nation should live through," he said, "a time of violence and tragedy."

After announcing the appointment of a special Advisory Commission on Civil Disorders, the president sought to give his assessment of the outbreaks and to appeal for self-examination on the part of all Americans.

In concluding statements, he called for positive action.

> Let us build something much more lasting: faith between man and man, faith between race and race, faith in each other—and faith in the promise of beautiful America.

> Let us pray for the day when mercy and truth are met together; righteousness and peace have kissed each other. Let us pray and let us work for better jobs and better housing and better education that so many millions of our own fellow Americans need so much tonight.

> Let us then act in the Congress, in the city halls, and in every community, so that this great land of ours may truly be "one nation under God with liberty and justice for all."

Following several weeks of studies and investigations, meeting in riot cities, and talking with many witnesses, the commission concluded that: "Our nation is moving toward two societies, one black, one white—separate and unequal." The only possible course for a sensible and humane nation, the commission argued, was "a policy which combines ghetto enrichment with programs designed to encourage integration of substantial numbers of Negroes into the society outside of the ghetto."

The commission recognized what the U.S. Supreme Court had acknowledged in 1954, that segregation had not produced equality of education, and consequently ruled that the separate-but-equal doctrine in public education was no longer constitutional.

Since the ruling, the district courts have demanded that school boards comply with the mandate of the Supreme Court. In cases where busing is the only tool adequate to achieve meaningful desegregation, the courts have recognized busing as a legitimate tool.

Obviously, with segregated neighborhoods, the neighborhood school concept will not desegregate schools except on a token basis. The freedom of choice plan, since it was initiated, has resulted in only a few blacks being assigned to white schools. Whites have failed to request assignment to black schools.

Regardless of how sincere the contention, those who still call for neighborhood schools and the elimination of busing as a tool to achieve desegregation of schools, are asking that the clock be turned back to the days prior to 1954. They are also overlooking the fact that busing was used extensively and effectively to maintain segregated schools. They are further saying, "Let's maintain two societies, one black, one white." And they are saying, "Abandon the goal of 'one nation under God with liberty and justice for all.'" In so doing, they are admitting that white America does not have the will or love to honestly work toward one community, thereby supporting the conclusion of the black separatists that integration is not a sincere desire of whites and that white racism still prevails in America.

Let us be aware that the Supreme Court has not only given a mandate. It has courageously offered a course for America to make good the promises of American democracy. The executive and legislative branches and white Americans can rebel and defeat gains that have been made in making America, in fact, "one nation."

In so doing, they are making democracy in America a mockery and the promises of liberty and justice for all a shattered dream for black people.

GREENSBORO: TWENTY-FIVE YEARS AFTER THE BROWN RULING

(Remarks made to the city school board at its March 28 meeting and published as an editorial in the Greensboro *News & Record*. The Rev. Otis L. Hairston Sr. was appointed to the Greensboro Board of Education in 1971)

According to the United States Commission on Civil Rights, nearly half of the nation's minority children still attend segregated schools.

Twenty-five years after the United States Supreme Court declared desegregation the law of the land, almost five million black and other minority students are enrolled in schools that are for the most part segregated and unequal.

Our nation has not had the will to abandon a system that breeds despair, hopelessness, degradation, and violence. We proclaim the creed but avoid the deed.

Although we favor quality education for all children, regardless of race, creed, color, or place of residence, we make no viable commitment to provide it.

In recent years, when busing has been ordered by the courts as an instrument to achieve desegregation, shouts of violent opposition and displeasure have been registered, although it was an acceptable instrument to maintain segregation.

Many of the citizens of Greensboro, who supported busing as a means of school segregation, perceive it today as a giant evil. Likewise, many of those who sought to maintain segregated communities call for community schools.

Following the court's Brown decision in 1954, the nation was focused on Greensboro. It was thought then that our city would make history as a progressive community.

The Board of Education was the first one in the South to announce that it would comply with the decision to desegregate its schools.

Most school board members recognized that the Supreme Court's decision was just and that desegregation provided the only means of achieving equal opportunity for quality education for all children.

The night after the decision was handed down, Mr. D. Edward Hudgins, chairman of the board, presented a resolution committing Greensboro to a policy of implementing the new law of the land. He urged fellow members neither to "fight or attempt to 'circumvent' it." Superintendent Benjamin Smith also supported the resolution. Both men felt that Greensboro had an opportunity to lead the South, even the nation.

Pressure from within and outside of Greensboro by those who were not ready to abandon segregated schools forced the board to defer implementation. As a result, our city was led to follow a "freedom of choice" plan advanced by Governor Luther Hodges. Although a few black students applied and were admitted to white schools, no white students requested to transfer to a black school.

It was not until 1972, as a result of a court mandate, that meaningful school desegregation occurred in Greensboro. The board wisely decided not to appeal the court's decision, but to bring the system in compliance with the law.

Today, we face a choice of whether to move toward quality education of all students or to continue to favor those who are termed "affluent."

The question now, as in former days, persists: "Should quality education be provided for every child in our school system regardless of race, creed, or place of residence?"

The time has come for us to make a commitment to guarantee to all of the students of the public schools of Greensboro an equal opportunity for quality education.

The time has come for us to request the money necessary to bring Lincoln and Dudley up to par with the other junior and senior high schools in other communities.

The time has come for us to demand that principals and teachers cease treating black and poor white students differently from the other students.

The time has come for citizens of Greensboro to be willing to be taxed to the extent necessary to equalize schools in all communities.

The time has come for every parent to seek the same opportunities for every child as he seeks for his own child.

The time has come for us to seek to do what is moral rather than what is expedient.

On July 27, 1967, President Lyndon B. Johnson addressed the nation after weeks of grave violence in many major cities of America. Violence had taken place for two summers on a wide scale. Concluding his speech, he called for positive action:

"Let us build faith between man and man, faith between race and race, faith in each other."

"Let us then act . . . in every community, so that this great land of ours may truly be one 'nation under God with liberty and justice for all.'"

Ralph Waldo Emerson once said that "This time, like all times, is a very good one, if we but know what to do with it."

God grant us the wisdom and the courage for these times that we might act wisely.

BLACK COLLEGES NEED SUPPORT

(Letter to the editor of the Greensboro *Daily News*)

During the months of November and December, Bennett College will sponsor its annual fundraising campaign on behalf of the United Negro College Fund. The campaign will involve people from various walks of life in the Greensboro area and will seek to raise the meager sum of $65,000.

It is imperative that the Greensboro area respond to this call to keep the forty-one colleges associated with the United Negro College Fund viable educational institutions. With many formerly black state-supported colleges being merged into university systems or closed, the need for private church-related colleges is greater than ever.

America owes a tremendous debt to the private black colleges. Through their influence and the leaders they have sent forth into the world, the cause of freedom and justice has been advanced and human dignity enhanced. The pioneer civil rights leaders were largely trained and inspired at church-related colleges.

Not only should we pay our debt for what these institutions have done, but we also need to support them sacrificially because of the significant role they can still play in producing and inspiring skillful and courageous, independent-thinking black leaders who will continue to make America uncomfortable with inequality and injustice. This is not only important for blacks but for our nation itself. "Where there is no vision, the people perish" (Prov. 29:18 KJV).

Let every one of us make an installment payment on our debt to the private black college within the next two months! For every dollar received in Greensboro, Bennett College will receive four dollars.

Keep the forty-one black church-related colleges viable through your liberal contributions.

PART V

Reprint of
A MANUAL
for Pulpit Search
Committees
in Baptist Churches
By Otis L. Hairston Sr.

PREFACE

This brief manual is written with the hope that it will be helpful to Baptist churches in their search for suitable pastors.

Our thanks to Dr. Howard A. Chubbs, pastor of Providence Baptist Church, Greensboro, North Carolina, and Dr. Leon C. Riddick, pastor emeritus of Mount Carmel Baptist Church, Charlotte, North Carolina, and former director of Christian education of the General Baptist State Convention of North Carolina for critiquing the initial draft; and Mrs. Ruby L. Widemon, retired secretary at the University of North Carolina at Greensboro and assistant clerk at Shiloh Baptist Church during most of my thirty-four years as pastor, for typing the first and final drafts.

The strongest and most successful minister is he or she who knows his or her weakness and who relies upon God for guidance and assistance.

—Walter R. Hazzard

THE PULPIT SEARCH COMMITTEE

One of the extremely difficult tasks a Baptist church is confronted with is that of calling a pastor. Perhaps the worst thing that can happen is to call a pastor who is not suited for the church and in a short period after assuming the pastorate is removed from office or chooses to leave the church.

Many churches have made tragic and costly mistakes in calling pastors. As a result, the health of the church has suffered.

It is important for pulpit search committees to secure information on how to search for a pastor. Guidelines and sound procedures ought to be approved by the committee before it starts its work.

This brief booklet is intended to offer information and suggestions on how the pulpit search committee in a Baptist church can approach and carry out its work effectively.

ON CALLING A PASTOR

(A statement from *The Hiscox Guide for Baptist Churches*)

"In calling a man to the pastorate, the church should take deliberate care to know his record; what he has done elsewhere, and how he is esteemed and valued where he has previously lived and labored. It is a folly of which churches are often guilty—and for which they justly suffer—that on the credit of a few flashy and fascinating sermons, wholly ignorant of his private character and of his ministerial history, they call and settle a pastor. A man of deep Christian commitment, thoroughly in love with the Word of God, is much to be preferred to the brilliant pulpiteer."

TWO THINGS NEEDED

Two things are very important as the church seeks to find the right person to lead the church in becoming all that Christ wants it to be.

First, the church must seek God's guidance in the search. It should always be the feeling that God alone knows the right minister for the church, and when the church earnestly prays, He will direct the search.

Second, the congregation needs to adopt sound procedures based on business principles but also on high Christian principles and practices. The procedures ought to be approved by the congregation itself rather than the search committee, the deacon board or the church council if one is in place.

THE CHURCH AT PRAYER

The first thing a church should do when the pulpit becomes vacant is to set aside a special period of prayer. The period should be at least a month. The entire congregation should be asked to pray daily for God's guidance. Special congregational prayers should be offered at all worship services.

An excellent scripture to be used throughout the search is Proverbs 3:5-6 KJV:

> Trust in the Lord with all thine heart, and lean not unto thine own understanding. In all thy ways acknowledge Him, and He shall direct thy paths.

Praying is important in seeking the direction of God, but also in keeping the church in unity during a most difficult period of its life.

A PERIOD OF TRAINING

After a period of prayer, the church should set aside at least three days within two weeks for two training sessions. The congregation should be made to fully understand what the church is up against as it searches for a pastor and the need for unity during the period. Emphasis should be placed on the need for a capable search committee and its work. The constitution or bylaws pertaining to calling a pastor should be fully discussed.

In the event the church does not have an approved constitution or bylaws, procedures for electing a pastor should be fully discussed. Some adopted procedure should be approved before the search committee is elected.

The training sessions should be conducted by someone who has experience in a pastoral search or by an experienced pastor in the area.

ELECTING THE SEARCH COMMITTEE

Electing members to serve on a pulpit search committee is a major task and should be done thoughtfully. Members should not be nominated on the basis of popularity or friendship but according to their usefulness.

It is a good practice to have the congregation elect members of the search committee in a duly called meeting.

Prior to the meeting, a decision should be made on the number of members to serve on the committee and how they will be nominated and voted on.

Some churches permit the deacon and trustee boards or the church council to nominate members of the committee to be voted on by the congregation. One advantage of this procedure is that thought is likely to be given of having the most useful persons nominated. Also, the committee will be representative of the membership.

Another procedure used is the nomination of persons from the floor during the congregational meeting. Whatever method is used, care should be given to have a committee that is representative of the church membership in terms of age, years in the church, diversity, and training. No two members of the same family should be elected to the committee.

Most churches find it helpful to have certain key officers of the church automatically on the committee: chairman of the deacon board, chairman of the trustee board, clerk of the church, superintendent of the Sunday school.

The search committee should always be voted on by the congregation in a duly called meeting. Notice of such meeting should be announced from the pulpit at least two Sundays prior to the meeting.

THE SIZE OF THE COMMITTEE

The size of the committee may be determined by the size of the membership of the church. Perhaps a church with a thousand or more members would more than likely want more committee members than a church with two hundred or fewer members. A committee, in either case, should not be too large to function well.

Generally, a committee should not exceed fifteen members in the larger churches or nine members in small churches.

Consideration should always be given to travel and meetings as the size of the committee is determined.

THE WORK OF THE COMMITTEE

The pulpit search committee is elected to assume leadership in finding a suitable pastor for the church and recommending him or her to the congregation.

It should be the practice of search committees to provide an opportunity for members of the congregation to express themselves on their conception of the kind of pastor the church needs, and a chance to meet the recommended pastor.

OFFICERS OF THE COMMITTEE

The chairman of the search committee should be elected by the congregation at the time it votes for members of the committee. It is important for the chairman to be a person highly respected by the members and with the ability to lead in organizing the committee for work. In the first meeting of the committee, a vice chairman should be chosen and a recording secretary. All of the meetings of the committee should be recorded by the secretary, made available to the chairman within a week, and read at the next meeting of the committee. All of the minutes recorded should be available at every meeting of the committee. All of the minutes should be safely kept throughout the period of its work.

The committee should always be aware of the seriousness of its responsibility and constantly and earnestly pray for God's guidance.

It is also important for the committee to project a time to complete its work. A schedule of meetings should be agreed upon at the first or second meeting of the committee, and each member of the committee should make a commitment to be faithful in attending meetings. No business of the committee should be conducted unless at least two-thirds of the committee are present.

SPECIFIC DUTIES

Specific duties should be outlined by the committee. They should include:

1. Developing a survey sheet for members to express their feelings on the kind of pastor the church needs.
2. Preparing a booklet giving a brief history of the church, its philosophy, the goals (short- and long-range), type of ministries carried on, organizations, its membership, building, special projects, convention affiliations, and the type of community and city in which the church is located.
3. Preparing a budget to be submitted to the committee disbursing expenditures.
4. Preparing questions for interviews with candidates.
5. Gathering names of prospective candidates.
6. Determining a method of evaluating, rating, and checking out candidates in regard to character, reputation, references, and achievement in current and past pastorates.

7. Arranging visits of candidates to the church, meet with members and serve as guest minister.
8. Recommending a candidate to the congregation.
9. Notifying a candidate when formally elected.
10. Preparing a news release when the new pastor accepts.
11. Making monthly reports to the congregation throughout the period of the search.

Sample of Questionnaire for Members on page 212.

Sample of Questions for final five candidates on page 213.

Some Questions for the Interview Session with top candidate on page 213.

THE SEARCH FOR CANDIDATES

An extremely important task of the committee is deciding the approach to use for finding and listing prospective candidates. Sound judgment must be used in deciding the source.

It has become a practice for churches to announce pulpit vacancies in denominational publications and to invite interested ministers to submit a résumé to the pulpit search committee. Some churches make the mistake of asking interested ministers to send in applications.

To request applications is out of line. The position of pastor should not be applied for. It is different than a position in industry, in institutions, in the job market.

When a church calls a pastor, it should be convinced that God has directed the pulpit search committee to the person. In one sense, the person has been chosen by God and elected by the congregation.

Another way to proceed in the search for a suitable candidate is to request deans and leaders of recognized theological seminaries to suggest ministers who have been successful pastors for three or more years as suitable candidates. Some pastors of larger churches could be interested. The informational booklet should be mailed with a request for recommendations.

A third way to secure names of suitable candidates is to ask national and state Baptist denominational leaders to submit names of ministers who have been successful as pastors of smaller churches and who may want a more challenging charge.

The opportunity should also be provided for members of the congregation to submit names and basic information of prospective candidates.

SMALLER CHURCHES SEEKING PASTORS

The size of a congregation, its location, and resources will play a great part in the type of pastor that a congregation can realistically hope to attract. While a smaller, rural, less well-funded congregation may not be able to attract a more experienced and highly trained pastor, it can still secure capable and often outstanding leadership. One source may be seminaries and schools of religion where young theological students have traditionally furnished excellent leadership and helped some smaller congregations to grow and succeed beyond their wildest expectations.

And, while formal training is always to be desired, we must be careful never to exclude from consideration other God-called ministers who have not yet had the benefit of a formal education but are serious students of the Word and determined to improve themselves and, by so doing, to render great service to "kingdom building" through service to the local church.

THE SCREENING PROCESS

After recommendations of candidates have been received from the various sources, the search committee should meet promptly and begin the screening process.

A folder should be prepared for each candidate containing his or her résumé, reference letters, and any other information furnished by him or her.

When ministers have been recommended by seminary deans, denominational leaders or pastors, it will be necessary to explore the interest of the persons recommended. It is possible that some of the ministers recommended by others will not want to be considered. Those who have interest should be asked to furnish résumés.

A list should be prepared of candidates who have expressed interest. As mentioned earlier, a folder should be prepared containing the résumé, reference letters, and other information secured.

It would be practical to appoint a small committee from the search committee to go through the folders and put aside those candidates who fail to meet the established requirements. For example, if a person must have a seminary degree to be considered, then those without the degree are automatically eliminated.

The entire committee would only need to go through folders of viable candidates (those qualified to be considered).

After a list of viable candidates has been completed and information received on them, the entire search committee should set up a rating system. The committee may want to rate candidates on their measuring up to the expectations expressed by members in the survey. A number-one rating would mean that the candidate completely fits the church expectation and desire. A number-two rating would indicate that the candidate closely fits the church's expectations and desires, and a number-three rating would indicate that the candidate poorly meets the expectations and desire of members.

The committee may want to use other measuring methods to rate candidates.

The screening process will eventually reduce the number of candidates to five. These ministers will be the ones who best meet the expectations and desire of the congregation. They will need to be completely investigated and their ministry assessed in terms of effectiveness.

SOME SUGGESTIONS FOR INVESTIGATING FINAL CANDIDATES

1. Reference letters and information on résumés should be verified.
2. A check should be made in the cities where the candidates have served to find out if they have criminal court records.
3. Visits to the candidates' churches by a small committee should be made unannounced.
4. Visits should be made to the communities of candidates for talks with business and community leaders. Barbershops and funeral homes are good places to visit.

Following the search committee's complete investigation of the final five candidates, the committee will need to meet and determine which candidate on the basis of the investigation, the visit to the church, and the evaluation of current and past ministry would best come up to the expectations and desires of congregation members and the committee. The minister would become the top candidate and the one the committee would meet with first.

The other four candidates should be ranked on the basis of how closely they meet the expectations and desires.

A meeting with the top candidate should be arranged as promptly as possible. The conference should be set for a time when the candidate and the committee can have ample time to deal with all the issues that must be discussed and resolved.

In this conference, the committee would not only interview the candidate, but the candidate should be given plenty of time to ask questions about the program, ministry, and goals of the church. The committee should inform the candidate of the expectations and desires expressed by members in a survey. It should also inform the candidate about the financial condition of the church and the amount in the budget for ministerial services.

After the interview, the committee should determine whether the candidate is the person it feels comfortable recommending as a pastor. In case the committee is not convinced that he is the best suited, it should feel free to arrange a meeting with the number-two candidate.

In the event the committee is satisfied with the top candidate, it should arrange to have him or her, and if possible his or her family, visit the church. An informal meeting could be arranged for a Saturday, providing members of the congregation a chance to meet the proposed pastor and his or her family.

On Sunday, the candidate would be provided the opportunity to conduct the worship service. Obviously, he would preach the sermon.

If the response is favorable after the meeting on Saturday and the service on Sunday, the search committee should ask the chairman of the deacon board to call a meeting of the congregation for the purpose of hearing a recommendation from the search committee and voting on a pastor.

THE CONGREGATIONAL MEETING

The congregational meeting to hear the recommendation of the pulpit search committee and to vote on the recommended candidate should be announced from the pulpit for two consecutive Sundays prior to the meeting.

In announcing the meeting, it should be made clear that the pulpit search committee will recommend a minister as pastor and the congregation will vote on the recommendation. There should be nothing else on the agenda for this special meeting.

The chairman of the deacon board is the presiding officer in church meetings in Baptist churches when the church is without the pastor. The only way to alter the procedure is for the congregation to elect a temporary moderator.

In preparing for the meeting of the congregation to vote for a pastor, ballots for voting should be prepared.

If the constitution or bylaws of the church fail to specify who is qualified to vote, it will be necessary to decide prior to the meeting who can vote. The decision should be firm.

Tellers will need to be appointed before the conference to be responsible for counting the ballots after the vote. The vote should be posted and the ballots kept for verification in case the vote is close and there is question. The clerk of the church should certify the outcome of the election and promptly notify the chairman of the pulpit search committee and the chairman of the deacon board.

With the certification of the election, the chairman of the search committee should immediately inform the elected pastor by telegram. The vote should be stated in the message.

AN EXAMPLE OF A MESSAGE
TO A NEWLY ELECTED PASTOR:

The congregation of _____Church today voted to extend you a call to be pastor by a vote of _____ to _____. A detailed letter of specifics will follow. The church anxiously awaits your response."

_____ Chairman, Search Committee
_____ Chairman, Deacon Board

The result of the vote should always be given in the notice of a call. No pastor would want to accept a call if the vote is by a slim margin. Many churches require a favorable vote of at least 66 percent of members voting.

Only after the elected pastor accepts the call should the news be released to the public through the news media.

With the acceptance, the pulpit search committee and the boards of the church should immediately start making arrangements for the new pastor's transition.

THE CONGREGATION'S RESPONSE

It is extremely important for the congregation to warmly receive its new pastor and his or her family.

Contact should be made with him or her to find out what assistance will be wanted from the church other than the normal assistance provided. It would be helpful to appoint a special committee to provide assistance throughout the transition. This committee should be primarily from the pulpit search committee. Members of the special committee should not be expected to render all of the services needed, but should be free to recruit members of the congregation to carry out specific jobs.

Finally, the congregation should be patient, kind, and tolerant with the new minister as he or she seeks to become adjusted to his or her new situation. Refrain from telling him or her that the former pastor did it "this way" or he or she "didn't do it that way." The new way could be a better way.

Above all, love him or her, support him or her, and pray constantly for him or her that he or she would be all that Christ wants him or her to be.

SURVEY SHEET FOR MEMBERS

Please check your preference in terms of a pastor.

1. What age person would you like as pastor?
    a. _____ 21-30;   b. _____ 31-40;   c. _____ 41-50;
    d. _____ Age doesn't matter.

2. What type of education should the pastor have?
    a. _____ College;   b. _____ Seminary;
    c. _____ Beyond Seminary;   d. _____ Training doesn't matter.

3. How much pastoral experience should the pastor have?
    a. _____ three years;   b. _____ five years;
    c. _____ five to ten years   d. _____ Over ten years.

4. What is your preference in terms of sex?
    a. _____ Male;   b. _____ Female;   c. _____ Gender doesn't matter.

5. Which three services do you feel are most important as a pastor?
    a._____ Administration
    b._____ Counseling
    c._____ Community Involvement
    d._____ Sick Visitation
    e._____ Preaching

f._____ Church Planning

g._____ Other

6. Would a single person (never married) be acceptable to you?
   _____ Yes _____ No

7. Would a divorced person be acceptable to you?
   _____ Yes _____ No

PROPOSED QUESTIONS FOR FINAL FIVE OR TEN CANDIDATES

1. How would you describe your leadership style?
2. How do you perceive the role of a pastor?
3. What are your views on a pastor's involvement in the community?
4. What do you consider the most important duty of a pastor?
5. Describe your early experience as a Christian.
6. How do you measure your success as a pastor?
7. What method do you use in evaluating the church itself?
8. What role should the pastor play in the financial management of the church?
9. What do you consider your greatest strength?
10. What do you consider your greatest weakness?

SOME QUESTIONS FOR AN INTERVIEW WITH THE TOP CANDIDATE

1. What do you consider the most important duty of a pastor?
2. When do you find time for personal meditation and prayer?
3. How much time do you spend with your family?
4. Name three of your closest friends.
5. What is your concept of the role of deacons in the church?

6. How do you perceive the role of youth members of the church?
7. What method of evangelism have you used in your ministry?
8. What are your primary goals as a pastor?
9. How do you determine the effectiveness of your preaching?
10. How do you feel about the church having a committee to evaluate your performance as a pastor?

THE AUTHOR

The Rev. Otis L. Hairston Sr. is pastor emeritus of Shiloh Baptist Church, Greensboro, North Carolina. He served as pastor from 1960 to 1993. Previously he served as assistant pastor for two years and also for eight years as pastor of Brookston Baptist Church, Henderson, North Carolina (a church with two hundred members).

POSITIONS HELD

Chairman of the Personnel Committee, General Baptist State Convention of North Carolina (four years)

Chairman of the Administrative Committee, General Baptist Convention (three years)

Chairman of the Trustee Affairs Committee, Shaw University Trustee Board (responsible for recommending trustees, two years)

SEARCH COMMITTEES

North Carolina Council of Churches' Search Committee

Shaw University Board of Trustees' Search Committee

Bennett College Board of Trustees' Search Committee

Greensboro Board of Education's Search Committee

Conductor of Association Workshop on Calling a Pastor

CONCLUSION

In April 2010, the groundbreaking ceremony for phase one of the Otis L. Hairston Family Life Center took place, and a dedication ceremony for the center was held on March 27, 2011. In a perfect world, the Rev. Hairston would have been there to walk through the halls, share his thoughts and visions on how this center could help members of the community, and move forward, shake the hands, and greet church and community members, teach a class on stewardship, or share in a meal and fellowship. The family life center, like the Otis L. Hairston Sr. Middle School, is symbolic of his legacy and the imprint he left on the Greensboro community.

The Rev. Hairston lived to serve God and His people. Each day his passion for living and his dedication were put into action through his ministry, giving back to those in need, and fighting for social justice.

This collection of sermons and writings reflects in the best sense who he was, what he lived for, and why his legacy is so important. The seeds for the call to service and commitment to making a difference, no matter how great or small, echo in the hearts of those who had the honor of knowing the Rev. Hairston. After reading this book, those who did not have the opportunity to know him will understand and appreciate the life of a humble Christian servant through his own words. We can all learn the importance of faith and the actions that truly help everyone put faith to work and bring meaning to life. The Rev. Hairston laid the foundation. We can all learn how to be a blessing to others. The Rev. Hairston embodied that sacred creed. We can all get a sense of our better selves and how to move forward in love, respect, compassion, faith, and a renewed purpose to serve through the *Words of a Good Shepherd*.

ABOUT THE AUTHOR/COMPILER

The Rev. Otis L. Hairston Sr. (1918-2000) lived for eighty-two wonderful years. His walk with God led him to develop a wealth of depth and understanding that he translated into inspirational messages every week for his congregation for forty years. He was a visionary and a man before his time, never satisfied to sit on the sidelines of history, but compelled to use his gifts, talents, and skills to serve God and others.

He graduated with a bachelor's degree in journalism in 1940 from Shaw University and later was awarded an honorary doctor of divinity degree by his alma mater. He served as pastor at Brookston Baptist Church in Henderson, North Carolina, for eight years and at Shiloh Baptist Church in Greensboro, North Carolina, for thirty-two years.

In 1981, Governor James B. Hunt conferred the Order of the Long Leaf Pine upon him with the title of ambassador extraordinary. He was awarded the 1983 Brotherhood Citation by the Greensboro chapter of the National Conference of Christians and Jews and in 1994 was enrolled in the Book of Golden Deeds by the Greensboro Exchange Club.

Emma Hairston Belle, compiler of this book, is the daughter of the Rev. Hairston. She received a bachelor's degree in music from the University of North Carolina at Greensboro in 1966. She is the mother of two daughters, Wanda Michelle Belle and Monica Warrenita Belle. She worked for nine years at the Library of Congress and recently retired from CareFirst of Maryland after twenty years. She resides in Randallstown, Maryland, with her husband, Dr. Melton P. Belle, daughter Monica and her mother, Anna C. Hairston.